THE

POCKET

IDIOT'S

GUIDE™ TO

Homemade
Dog Food

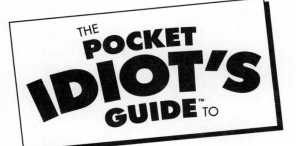

THE POCKET IDIOT'S GUIDE™ TO

Homemade Dog Food

by Margaret H. Bonham

ALPHA

A member of Penguin Group (USA) Inc.

ALPHA BOOKS

Published by the Penguin Group

Penguin Group (USA) Inc., 375 Hudson Street, New York, New York 10014, USA

Penguin Group (Canada), 90 Eglinton Avenue East, Suite 700, Toronto, Ontario M4P 2Y3, Canada (a division of Pearson Penguin Canada Inc.)

Penguin Books Ltd, 80 Strand, London WC2R 0RL, England

Penguin Ireland, 25 St. Stephen's Green, Dublin 2, Ireland (a division of Penguin Books Ltd.)

Penguin Group (Australia), 250 Camberwell Road, Camberwell, Victoria 3124, Australia (a division of Pearson Australia Group Pty. Ltd.)

Penguin Books India Pvt. Ltd., 11 Community Centre, Panchsheel Park, New Delhi—110 017, India

Penguin Group (NZ), 67 Apollo Drive, Rosedale, North Shore, Auckland 1311, New Zealand (a division of Pearson New Zealand Ltd.)

Penguin Books (South Africa) (Pty.) Ltd, 24 Sturdee Avenue, Rosebank, Johannesburg 2196, South Africa

Penguin Books Ltd., Registered Offices: 80 Strand, London WC2R 0RL, England

Copyright © 2007 by Penguin Group (USA) Inc.

International Standard Book Number: 978-1-59257-739-2
Library of Congress Catalog Card Number: 2007930861

09 08 07   8 7 6 5 4 3 2 1

Interpretation of the printing code: The rightmost number of the first series of numbers is the year of the book's printing; the rightmost number of the second series of numbers is the number of the book's printing. For example, a printing code of 07-1 shows that the first printing occurred in 2008.

Printed in the United States of America

Note: This publication contains the opinions and ideas of its author. It is intended to provide helpful and informative material on the subject matter covered. It is sold with the understanding that the author and publisher are not engaged in rendering professional services in the book. If the reader requires personal assistance or advice, a competent professional should be consulted.

The author and publisher specifically disclaim any responsibility for any liability, loss, or risk, personal or otherwise, which is incurred as a consequence, directly or indirectly, of the use and application of any of the contents of this book.

Most Alpha books are available at special quantity discounts for bulk purchases for sales promotions, premiums, fund-raising, or educational use. Special books, or book excerpts, can also be created to fit specific needs.

For details, write: Special Markets, Alpha Books, 375 Hudson Street, New York, NY 10014.

To Larry, as always.

Contents

Introduction

Since dogs and humans got together some 20,000 years ago, people have been feeding their dogs. Much of the time, the dogs ate what scraps people didn't want, but many dogs received food in the form of vegetables, meat, and grains.

Commercial dog food is a relatively new phenomenon. The first commercial dog food appeared in the form of a biscuit in the mid-1800s. Since then, dog food manufacturers have enjoyed a monopoly on feeding dogs in today's society. And little wonder—feeding dogs from cans or bags of kibble is convenient. And within the last 30 years, commercial dog food has been quite a bit better than what most people had been feeding their dogs, that is, table scraps.

However, there's been a new movement in feeding our dogs. Scares about ingredients in commercial pet foods have led many people to look hard at commercial food and ask if that's really what they want to feed their best friends.

This book looks at how to feed your dog with homemade dog food. It isn't a substitute for a veterinary nutritionist or a veterinarian—who should be monitoring your dog's diet and health at all times. The recipes in this book won't perform miracles overnight and none are intended to be fed as the only source of nutrition. Still, it's a way for you to care for your dog and have fun at the same time.

Extras

In addition to the main text, this book includes five types of sidebars, each with a distinctive visual cue.

Treats

These are tips that will help you feed your dog more easily.

No Biscuit!

These are warnings—stuff you need to pay attention to.

Definition

These are definitions of words you might not have known.

Yummy Snacks

These are things that maybe you didn't know and might be of some interest to you.

Home Cookin'

These are the recipes. Try them!

Acknowledgments

I want to thank Anne Page, Karen Holowinski, Charlene LaBelle, and Jessica Allen for recipes. I also want to thank Randy Ladenheim-Gil and Mike Sanders for giving me the opportunity to write this book. I want to thank my agent, Jessica Faust at Bookends. Last, I want to thank my dogs and my husband, Larry, for putting up with the screwy schedule to get this book completed.

Trademarks

Chapter 1

Should You Make Your Own Dog Food?

In This Chapter

- The problems with commercial dog food
- Reasons for staying with commercial dog food
- Types of diets available

You've picked up this book wondering whether you should feed your dog a commercial diet or whether you should be making your dog's food yourself. This chapter discusses the pros and cons of making your dog's food and whether you should try to feed your dog a homemade diet.

What's Wrong with Commercial (Store-Bought) Food?

If you're just a little in tune with the news, you probably already know what's wrong with today's commercial dog food. Problems with the quality of ingredients, questions as to whether the food is really good for your dog, and issues with adequate nutrition have made people rethink their pet food choices. The situation with Menu Foods and the potentially contaminated *wheat gluten* in pet food has made people look long and hard at their choice of pet food. When so many dog and cat foods have been affected, you may be wondering if pet food is indeed safe.

On one side are the people in the pet food industry and those who still believe in commercial pet foods. These people will tell you that for the most part, pet food is very safe, and the convenience, price, and nutritional value far outweigh the risk factors. On the other side are people who will not feed commercial food to their pets for any reason, making allegations that commercial food causes cancer, is made up of road kill and dead pets, and can't be good for your dog. They point to the melamine contamination and other problems that have been associated with commercial pet foods, and conclude that no commercial pet food can be good.

Definition

Wheat gluten is a type of protein derived from wheat.

The **FDA** (U.S. Food and Drug Administration) is the Federal Government's regulatory agency that supervises food, animal feed, and medications for safety in the United States.

The reality of the statements made about commercial versus homemade pet food lies somewhere in the middle. While not all commercial pet foods are bad, some are, and most pet food manufacturers are subject to the vagaries of ingredient suppliers. Unless the manufacturer supervises the production of each ingredient, there's a chance for tainted and bad ingredients to slip through even the most rigorous quality control and testing. (Melamine, for example, slipped through quality testing because it wasn't perceived as a common contaminant.) Because the *FDA* currently can only inspect around 2 percent of shipments imported into the United States, it's likely that there will be other contaminants found in commercial dog food for years to come.

Yummy Snacks

What some people have now called the "Pet Food Crisis of 2007" had to do with contaminated wheat gluten that came from China that was used in "cuts and gravy"-style canned food. The current belief is that the wheat gluten (and later discovered, rice protein) was contaminated with a plastic substance called melamine that was used at one time in kitchen utensils but has since been banned in the United States. Another ingredient, cyanuric acid, was found in the food, and the two combined with deadly results in some animals. It appeared to cause renal failure mostly in cats, but some dogs were affected as well.

Easy Biscuits

My dogs love this easy biscuit recipe. It's simple to make and is made with human-quality ingredients that you can eat, too, if you're so inclined.

2 cubes beef, chicken, or vegetable bouillon*	1 cup cornmeal
1 stick butter	1 cup nonfat dried milk
1 cup boiling hot water*	1 egg
3 cups whole-wheat flour	1 TB. dried parsley (optional)

*Note: You can substitute chicken or beef broth for the water and bouillon.

1. Preheat oven to 350°F. In a large bowl, mix bouillon, butter, and hot water until dissolved. Add flour, cornmeal, and nonfat dried milk. Mix well. Add egg and parsley, and mix. Dough should be thick but not dry. Add extra flour or water as needed and knead with hands.

2. Roll dough out on floured surface and cut with bone-shaped cookie cutter. Put on ungreased cookie sheet and bake one hour until bottom is browned or until hard. Remove and cool. Store in airtight containers.

Not to be used as a dog's only food.

Reasons to Make Your Own Dog Food

There are various reasons to make your dog's food. These include the following:

🦴 **Wanting to control the ingredients in your dog's food.** In many cases, pet owners want to take charge of their dog's diet and make sure the dog is getting all the proper nutrition she needs. They also want to be sure that the ingredients in the dog's food are healthy and of a similar quality to the food they would eat.

Treats

There's good news when it comes to balancing homemade dog food. There's a product formulated by a veterinary nutritionist that is called Balance-It. It's available through www.balanceit.com, and it provides the nutrition your dog needs in a homemade diet. There are other supplements out on the market for homemade dog foods, so be sure to use ones developed by veterinary nutritionists.

🦴 **Having to feed a particularly picky eater who will not eat commercial dog food.** In many cases, pet owners have turned to making their own dog food because their dog is a picky eater and doesn't like the taste of commercial dog food.

- ❧ **Needing to feed your dog a special diet for health reasons.** Some pet owners have pets who must follow special diets—they're allergic to specific ingredients or they have heart or kidney problems.

- ❧ **Lack of preservatives.** We know that some preservatives are bad for us, so eliminating the preservatives is easier when making our dog's food.

- ❧ **Enjoying doing something special for your dog.** Because dogs love homemade food, the owners enjoy cooking for their dogs.

These are all valid reasons for wanting to make your dog's own food.

No Biscuit!

It's very tempting to think that you can just whip up a few eggs, some chicken and vegetables, and call it a balanced meal for your dog, but nothing could be further from the truth. All diets—including what you feed your dog from this book—should be evaluated by a veterinary nutritionist for possible deficiencies.

Karen's Yummy Veggies

This is a great recipe to add to your dog's meals. My sister regularly gives this to her German Shepherd, who loves this with her special diet.

1 (32 oz.) bag frozen green beans	¼ cup water
	1 lb. baby carrots

1. Put green beans in a microwave-safe bowl, add water, and microwave on high five minutes or until tender. Drain, set aside, and let cool.

2. Wash baby carrots and run through a food processor with a dice, julienne, or slicing attachment.

3. In a large bowl, mix carrots and cooled green beans. Bag and freeze for later use. Feed ¼ cup to small dogs, ½ cup to medium dogs, and 1 to 2 cups to large dogs.

Not to be used as a dog's only food.

Reasons to Buy Commercially Prepared Food

So we know why you should make your own food. But are there any reasons your dog should stick with a commercial diet? Well, yes. Actually, there are plenty of good reasons for using a commercial diet, even though there are many reasons not to.

Here are some valid reasons for feeding your dog a commercial diet:

- 🦴 **Convenience.** It takes less time to pour kibble in a bowl or open a can of dog food than it does to make your dog's food. This is important if you have a very busy schedule.

- 🦴 **Nutritional adequacy.** Many homemade diets are not complete and balanced for dogs. On the other hand, commercial dog food with an *AAFCO* adequacy statement, meaning that the food is complete and balanced, can be fed to a dog daily and provide all the nutrition that your dog needs.

Definition

AAFCO (the Association of Animal Feed Control Officials) is made up of veterinarians, state feed-control officials, and pet food manufacturers who have developed guidelines for nutritional adequacy in pet foods.

- 🦴 **Travel and boarding.** It's harder to get pet sitters and boarding kennels to whip up something for your dog when you're gone.

- 🦴 **Less chance of spoilage and bacteria.** While bacteria may inhabit commercial fresh and frozen pet foods, most kibble and canned foods stay fresh for six months to a year.

- 🦴 **Cost.** Commercial food is usually far cheaper than buying your own ingredients and putting them together.

These are all good reasons for keeping your dog on a commercial diet.

Rover's Brunch for Two

Who says you can't share your breakfast with your pup? You and your dog can have brunch together, if you're so inclined. You can substitute your favorite fixings, if you wish. (See Chapter 4 for information on avoiding poisonous vegetables, fruits, and nuts and you'll be okay.)

2 TB. oil (canola, flax-seed, or olive)
1 or 2 cooked chicken breasts, deboned, cut into bite-size pieces
Your choice of veggies cut into bite-size pieces (carrots, broccoli, cauliflower, green peppers, kale, celery, and so on)

6 eggs
⅛ tsp. salt
½ tsp. dried parsley
½ cup shredded cheese (any variety)

1. Heat skillet with 1 TB. oil. Mix chicken and choice of vegetables, and toss into the skillet, sautéing until vegetables are tender and chicken is warm. Remove from skillet and set aside.

2. Beat eggs with salt and parsley. Mix in half of shredded cheese. Add 1 TB. oil and pour half of egg mixture into the hot skillet. Cook egg as you would for an omelet, pushing cooked egg to the center of the skillet and letting the uncooked portions flow into the pan to be cooked.

continues

3. When egg is cooked, put half the vegetable and chicken mixture on one side of the omelet, sprinkle with half of remaining cheese, and fold. Flip omelet and continue to cook until cheese is melted. Remove from skillet onto plate and let cool for your dog while you make the second omelet in the same fashion for yourself.

For small dogs, you'll want to cut the omelet in thirds and feed one portion per breakfast. Medium dogs can get a half omelet and large dogs can have a full omelet. Add balancing supplements such as Balance-It or those developed by your veterinarian to the food to ensure proper nutrition. Put any unused omelet in an airtight container and store in the refrigerator and use by the next day. You may want to add a couple of homemade biscuits such as Easy Biscuits for fiber.

Not to be used as a dog's only food.

In Between—If You Want to Do a Bit of Each

The other option for feeding your dog is to do a little bit of each—that is, feed your dog a premium commercial diet but still add some home-cooked additions. This may be the best of both worlds, as your dog will get the nutrition he needs and you can still feed your dog some yummy snacks.

I've known plenty of dog owners who decide on this option because they still lead busy lives but want to be sure that their dogs get the right nutrition. These people often choose organic commercial diets that use human-grade ingredients—and many of their diets are often frozen or freeze-dried commercial raw diets as well. These owners tend to look for organic diets because the food is less likely to have meat with growth hormones or residuals of pesticides.

The downside to mixing both is that you can cause an imbalance in your dog's diet if you overdo it. This is why it's important to have a good grasp on nutrition when making your own diet or mixing commercial and homemade. Try to keep the fat and sodium to a minimum, and stick with lean meats and fruits and vegetables.

Treats

Here are some easy snacks or additions to your dog's kibble: uncooked baby carrots, sliced celery, sliced bananas, diced hard-boiled eggs, cooked lean meat, cottage cheese, plain yogurt, canned pumpkin, or cooked sweet potatoes.

Commercial Raw and Organic Diets

Let's say that you're a little squeamish about creating your own diet for your dog, but you still want the benefits you can get from feeding your dog a homemade cooked or raw diet. Can you still do this?

If you're feeding your dog a raw diet, there are several good frozen raw diets available that are complete and balanced according to AAFCO standards. Likewise, there are many good natural and organic diets available.

The trick to purchasing pet food is to find out the quality control of the product. Pet food companies may or may not have strict control over the source of their ingredients, which will make a difference as to whether the food might be contaminated. Also, knowing the company has good quality control practices will help to ensure their food is not contaminated or spoiled.

No Biscuit!

Just because the company touts itself as "natural" or "organic" is no guarantee of quality. Some natural pet food companies were affected by contaminated Chinese wheat gluten in their products. Contact the company to find out their quality control methods and suppliers.

Basic Food Mix for Dogs

There are plenty of basic meals for dogs out there; however, many aren't as balanced as they need to be. When making dog food, be sure to use a balancing supplement and have a veterinary nutritionist analyze the food for any deficiencies.

Yield: 3 meals for a 60 lb. dog

2 cups white rice	1 cup cottage cheese
4 cups water	2 hardboiled eggs, peeled and diced
1 tsp. dried parsley	
1 tsp. salt	1 tsp. bone meal
1 lb. hamburger (80/20)	Balance-It or other supplement
⅓ cup liver, cut up into small pieces	

1. Add rice, water, parsley, and salt to a pan, then cover and bring to a boil. Turn to low heat and cook until all water is absorbed.

2. In the meantime, take hamburger and liver, and sauté them in a skillet until thoroughly cooked. Let cool.

3. In a mixing bowl, add rice and meat, and mix well. Let cool. Mix in cottage cheese, egg, bone meal, and Balance-It (according to directions). Put in airtight containers and refrigerate or freeze.

4. When ready to feed, split the food in thirds. Use within two days if refrigerated, or within a month if frozen.

Not to be used as a dog's only food.

The Least You Need to Know

- Homemade dog food enables you to control the ingredients and nutritional value of your dog's food.

- Homemade food must be properly balanced in order to not cause deficiencies or vitamin toxicity.

- There are supplements made to balance homemade dog food, such as Balance-It.

- If you're not comfortable just feeding homemade dog food to your dog, try mixing commercial dog food with some of your homemade foods.

2

Raw Versus Home-Cooked— Types of Diets Out There

In This Chapter

- 🦴 Raw or home-cooked diets—which makes sense?
- 🦴 Basic raw and cooked diets
- 🦴 Are table scraps okay?

You're now thinking that a homemade diet is the way to feed your dog. But which diet is best for you and your dog? In this chapter, we talk about the pros and cons of raw and cooked diets—and which ones are the best for your dog.

Raw or Home-Cooked—Which is Better?

If you've been on the Internet, you've probably heard about raw diets, especially the BARF (Biologically Appropriate Raw Food) diet as developed by Ian Billinghurst.

The basic premise is this: dogs came from wolves and wolves eat raw meat, bones, organ meats, and the contents of ruminants in the wild. Raw diets are much more natural than kibble or canned dog food.

There's a lot to be said for this. If you offer raw meat to your dog, she's likely to wolf it down (pun intended) rather than eat a bowl of kibble. (Of course, there are dogs who would gobble up the meat and then inhale the kibble, too, but that's beside the point.) But is raw meat better than cooked meat?

Yummy Snacks

The reason for keeping the meat raw is vitamins are destroyed if the meat is cooked. Raw meat has less processing and therefore is more natural. Raw bones are less hazardous than cooked bones and can often go through the digestive tract with little or no problem.

Raw Diets: Pros and Cons

Well, raw is sometimes better than cooked. We'll look at the benefits first before getting into the caveats about raw diets. Here are the benefits to raw diets:

- Raw diets are more natural than cooked or kibble diets.
- Raw bones are safer and less likely to cause perforations in intestinal tracts than cooked bones.

- Raw bones keep teeth cleaner than kibble or cooked diets do.
- Raw diets contain a better source of natural vitamins and minerals than cooked diets or kibble.
- They require less preparation time than home-cooked diets.
- Raw diets are also commercially available.

There's a lot of anecdotal evidence that points to raw diets being so much better than commercial diets. Many pet owners who feed raw diets claim that their pets have healthier coats and more energy than they did on commercial dog food. But like most things, these diets have detriments, too. Some of the issues with raw diets include the following:

- Raw diets can be a source of dangerous bacteria such as E. coli, salmonella, and campylobacter. While many dogs seem to handle these bacteria, you can contract these bacteria from your dog because he ingests them. Dogs can and do get sick from bacteria, and while uncommon, it's common enough to make note of it.
- Raw bones can still be lethal to pets. Many a veterinarian has had to remove bone blockages from pets.
- Some raw diets recommend feeding your pet entire dead animals, such as chickens, goats, or whatever. The stench of decaying

animals in your backyard may be enough to dissuade you from feeding this way (not to mention the bacteria and maggots!).

No Biscuit!

Because of the dangers of contracting a bacterial infection, you need to be extra careful when fixing raw meat for your dog. Always wear latex or other protective gloves when handling the meat, and keep the meat frozen until use. Throw out any portions of meat that haven't been eaten or that have been sitting at room temperature longer than an hour.

- Some raw meats, such as raw salmon (lung fluke) and raw pork (trichinosis), are dangerous due to parasites. Other raw meats coming from game may carry roundworms.

- Some raw diets purport to be more natural, but many of the foods are unlikely to have been in a wolf's diet at any time. (Since when does a wolf have access to green beans, lettuce, and bok choy?)

- Care must be taken in handling raw meat in order for you to avoid getting sick from bacteria and also to prevent spoilage.

The major issue that some veterinary nutritionists have with raw diets is the danger of bacterial infections. Because of this, many recommend cooking your dog's food and adding the appropriate supplements back in.

Cooked Diets: Pros and Cons

What about cooked diets? Well, there are benefits as well as caveats to the cooked diets. Let's look at the benefits first:

- 🦴 Cooked diets are generally safer because bacteria are more likely to be destroyed through the cooking process.
- 🦴 Cooking usually makes dangerous meat safer by killing parasites.
- 🦴 Cooked foods are usually as palatable as raw foods.
- 🦴 Food may be easier to digest due to the cooking process.

Like anything, these diets also have detriments. Here are the pitfalls of cooked foods:

- 🦴 Nutrition is lost through the cooking process and must be added.
- 🦴 Cooked bones are more dangerous to feed your dogs; in fact, you should never feed small cooked bones to dogs.
- 🦴 Care is still required when handling and cooking food.

Treats

The basic problem with cooking bones is that the bones can become very hard and brittle, and are thus not as digestible as raw bones. This is why it's important to never give cooked bones to your dog.

So which diets are really better? Should you go with raw food and potentially take the risk of giving your dog or yourself a serious bacterial infection? Or do you cook the food at home and add all the right nutrition to it? It's really up to you, but for safety's sake, I recommend cooking food and adding supplements as required.

Carrot Cake for Dogs

A friend of mine recommends modifying a carrot cake recipe suitable for dogs. Note there's no sugar, raisins, or frosting. This makes a great treat for a dog party.

4 eggs	2 tsp. baking soda
1¼ cups vegetable oil	2 tsp. baking powder
2 tsp. vanilla extract	½ tsp. salt
2¼ cups all-purpose flour	2 tsp. ground cinnamon
	3 cups grated carrots

1. Preheat oven to 350°F. Grease a 9×13 pan. Beat together eggs, oil, and vanilla. Add flour, baking soda, baking powder, salt, and cinnamon. Fold in carrots.

2. Bake for 50 minutes or until a wooden toothpick comes out clean testing from center. Cut into squares and serve.

Not to be used as a dog's only food.

Basic Raw Diets (BARF and Others)

The concept behind raw food diets for dogs is that raw food diets provide a more natural diet to one's dog, similar to what wolves might eat in the wild. There are countless raw diets, many of similar design, but there are enough differences to mention a few of the more famous ones:

- **BARF or "Biologically Appropriate Raw Food" Diet.** This diet was made popular by Dr. Ian Billinghurst. About 60 percent of the diet is raw meaty bones and the rest is a variety of vegetables and supplements. It is very popular.

- **The Natural Diet by Wendy Volhard (or the Volhard Diet).** This diet is primarily based on meat combined with grains, vitamins, and various healthy foods such as yogurt, liver, and wheat germ.

- Whole Prey Diet. In this diet, you give the dog a whole animal carcass to eat—skin, bones, hair, hooves, and all. The idea is that this is closest to what a dog would eat in the wild.

There are other raw diets out there—too numerous to list. The best recommendation I can make is to bring the diets to your veterinarian or a veterinary nutritionist and have them evaluated.

Peanut Butter Biscuits

½ cup butter, melted
2 eggs
1 cup peanut butter
1 cup nonfat dried milk

4 cups whole-wheat flour
1 cup water

1. Preheat oven to 350°F. Cream butter and eggs. Add peanut butter and then mix. Add nonfat dried milk, flour, and enough of the water until it is a doughy consistency.

2. Roll into balls or cut into cookies and place on baking sheet. Bake until brown, about one hour. Store in an airtight container or in plastic freezer bags and freeze. Makes for yummy treats.

Not to be used as a dog's only food.

Treats

Almost all treats need to stay in the freezer or in airtight containers and need to be used quickly, or you run the risk of spoiling them.

Basic Cooked Diets

What about cooked diets? Well, the good news is that you can take any raw diet and cook it. You'll have to avoid cooking bones and instead substitute bone meal or calcium in the form of powdered dried eggshells. You can also try a plethora of different recipes to suit both your dog's and your palate.

The main issue with cooked diets is that you will destroy many of the vitamins that your dog would get in raw diets. The trick is to add those vitamins with a supplement intended to make the diet balanced.

The nifty thing about cooked diets is that many human recipes can be adapted for dogs. So when you're making breakfast-type stuff, you may want to adapt recipes you love for your dog.

Liver Bars

This recipe is great with meals that need extra vitamins. These can spoil fast, so be sure to keep them in the freezer until you use them.

3 lbs. liver, ground up using a food processor	1 cup white flour
	3 cups whole-wheat flour

1. Preheat to 350°F. Use a nonstick cooking spray on the pan and dust with flour. Mix liver and white flour. Mix in whole-wheat flour until the mixture is thick and the consistency of dough.
2. Bake 45 minutes or until no longer pink. Cut into bars.

Not to be used as a dog's only food.

What About Table Scraps?

In the past, it was very common to give dogs table scraps as part of their meals. Dogs often love table scraps because they're chock full of fat, salt, sugar, carbohydrates, and other things that your dog just doesn't need. Think of table scraps as a dog's junk food. If you do, you'll understand why I recommend that no more than 5 percent of a dog's calories should come from table scraps.

No Biscuit!

The basic problem of feeding a dog table scraps is that the scraps are often loaded with fat, salt, sugar, and starch—most of which your dog doesn't need. Most table scraps are low in the vitamins a dog needs and are far from being balanced. If you want to home-cook your dog's food, skip the scraps.

When you do feed your dog table scraps, think about what is most healthy for your dog. Lean bits of cooked meat are good, as are cooked veggies, provided that you went light on the fat and salt. Remember that not all human food is good for your dog, so stay away from onions, grapes, raisins, chocolate, macadamia nuts, bones, and other potentially perilous food (see Chapter 4 for a more complete list of foods dangerous for your dog).

Good Morning Sunshine Muffins for Dogs

This is a nice treat for your dog. A muffin (or part of a muffin) along with yogurt or cottage cheese and cooked eggs would be a welcome breakfast for any pooch. And who knows? Maybe you'll like it, too.

2½ cups water
½ cup unsweetened applesauce
1 egg
¼ tsp. vanilla
1 tsp. cinnamon

1 TB. baking powder
4 cups whole-wheat flour
1 cup diced apples
½ cup sunflower seeds (shelled)

1. Preheat oven to 375°F. Spray muffin tins with nonstick spray. Mix water, applesauce, egg, vanilla, cinnamon, and baking powder. Add whole-wheat flour, diced apples, and sunflower seeds.

2. Bake for one hour or until toothpick comes out clean. Cool on racks and store in airtight bags in freezer.

Not to be used as a dog's only food.

Banana Muffins for Dogs

2 large eggs
1 cup mashed ripe bananas
1 cup buttermilk
1 cup wheat bran
¼ cup oil
1 tsp. vanilla extract

1 cup whole-wheat flour
¾ cup white flour
1½ tsp. baking powder
½ tsp. baking soda
½ tsp. ground cinnamon
¼ tsp. salt

1. Preheat oven to 400°F. Mix eggs, bananas, buttermilk, wheat bran, oil, and vanilla together.

2. Mix dry ingredients together, then add to wet ingredients until thoroughly mixed. Grease muffin cups and scoop into cups. Bake 25 minutes until brown. Let cool. Store in airtight freezer bags until use.

Not to be used as a dog's only food.

The Least You Need to Know

- There are many raw diets available, both store-bought and homemade.

- Cooked food is generally safer than raw. There are many different diets available, and you can cook raw diets to make them safer.

- You can modify favorite human recipes to fit your dog's diet.

Chapter 3

Nutrition Basics

In This Chapter

- 🦴 Learn what nutrients are necessary for a healthy dog
- 🦴 Protein, fat, and carbohydrates and the roles they play in a dog's health and energy
- 🦴 Vitamins and minerals that a dog needs

You know that nutrition is very important for your dog, but what nutrition does your dog actually need? What are protein, fat, and carbohydrates, and what role do they play in your dog's metabolism?

And just as important as protein, fat, and carbohydrates are vitamins and minerals. It's important to understand their roles in a dog's metabolism as well as the links between certain minerals.

In this chapter, we look at the role vital nutrients play in a dog's health. We also discuss what happens when a vitamin deficiency occurs, or when a dog is given too much (some vitamins are toxic).

What are AAFCO Guidelines?

Let's first take a look at AAFCO guidelines. Many folks who make their own dog food are quick to point out that AAFCO guidelines contain the bare minimum nutrition to keep a dog alive—and I agree. However, it's a good beginning because if you're not at least meeting AAFCO guidelines, you're probably causing some serious imbalances.

According to AAFCO guidelines, puppy food must have 22 percent protein and adult food must have 18 percent protein on a *dry-matter basis* as a minimum requirement. Puppy food must have 8 percent fat and adult food must have 5 percent fat on a dry-matter basis as a minimum requirement. There is no requirement for carbohydrates, although carbohydrates are still important in a dog's diet, as you will see.

Definition

Dry-matter basis is the percentage or amount of nutrient as compared to the overall weight of the food without water.

AAFCO Minimums for Vitamins in Dry-Matter (mg/kg)

Vitamins	Puppy and Adult Food
Vitamin A	1.5 (15 max)
Vitamin D	.00125 (.125 max)

Vitamins	Puppy and Adult Food
Vitamin E	50 (1,000 max)
Thiamine	1.0
Riboflavin	2.2
Pantothenic Acid	10
Niacin	11.4
Pyridoxine	1.0
Folic Acid	.18
Vitamin B12	.022
Choline	1,200

AAFCO Minimums and Maximums for Minerals in Dry-Matter

Minerals	Units (min/max)	Puppy (min/max)	Adult
Calcium	g/kg	10/25	6/25
Phosphorus	g/kg	8/16	5/16
Ca/P ratio		1:1/2:1	1:1/2:1
Potassium	g/kg	6	6
Sodium	g/kg	3	.6
Chloride	g/kg	4.5	.9
Magnesium	g/kg	.4/3	.4/3
Iron	mg/kg	80/3,000	80/3,000
Copper	mg/kg	7.3/250	7.3/250
Manganese	mg/kg	5	5
Zinc	mg/kg	120/1,000	120/1,000
Iodine	mg/kg	1.5/50	1.5/50
Selenium	mg/kg	.11/2	.11/2

But what does this all mean? Basically, this is the level of nutrients your dog needs to be getting in order to thrive. Without this level of nutrients, your dog will most likely have health problems. Some of these problems, such as a calcium and phosphorus imbalance, may take months or even years before the signs show. And then it may be too late. This is why it's very important to have a veterinary nutritionist analyze your dog's diet. We'll talk more about this later.

Doing Better Than AAFCO

So you've looked over the vitamins and minerals and wonder if perhaps you can do better than AAFCO. Most definitely! Many people do, and they have very healthy dogs. The main thing to keep in mind is to keep the levels of vitamins and minerals within the recommended limits and work with the freshest food possible.

The Essential Nutrients

What exactly *is* the proper nutrition? Dogs require energy in the form of *calories* or *kilocalories*. The nutrients that provide energy are proteins, fats, and carbohydrates. Dogs also need vitamins and minerals to maintain good health. Last, but certainly not least, dogs need water—the most vital of nutrients. Dogs can go for days without food, but begin to deteriorate rapidly without water. All of these nutrients are essential for a dog's survival.

Definition

A **calorie** is a measure of energy. It is the energy required to raise the temperature of a gram of water by 1° Centigrade.

A **kilocalorie** is the energy required to raise the temperature of a kilogram of water by 1° Centigrade.

Proteins (Meat)

Protein is an essential nutrient. It provides 4 kilocalories per gram and provides the building blocks for muscles, bone, organs, and connective tissue. It is the main component of enzymes, hormones, and antibodies. It aids in repairing muscle, building and maintaining plasma volume and red blood cells, and building mitochondrial volume in working dogs.

Protein is composed of 23 different *amino acids*. Of these 23, a dog's body can manufacture 13 (otherwise known as *nonessential amino acids*). The other 10 amino acids, called *essential amino acids*, must come from a dog's nutrition.

Definition

Amino acids are the building blocks that make up protein.

Nonessential amino acids are amino acids that are manufactured within a dog's body.

Essential amino acids are amino acids that must be present in a dog's diet to prevent a deficiency.

The essential amino acids are arginine, histidine, isoleucine, leucine, lysine, methionine, phenylalanine, threonine, tryptophan, and valine. A protein source with all 10 amino acids is said to be a *complete protein source*. Protein sources without all 10 are said to be *incomplete protein sources*.

Definition

A **complete protein source** is a source of protein that contains all 10 essential amino acids.

An **incomplete protein source** is a source of protein that contains only nine or less of the essential amino acids.

The amino acids must be balanced in such a way that the dog gets enough protein for her body. A combination of plant and animal sources usually offers the most complete diet. Because dogs are carnivores, they digest and use protein from animal products better than from plant sources. Good sources of protein include meat (chicken and poultry included), eggs, and meat by-products such as *offal*.

Definition

Offal are organ meats and intestines.

Fats

Fat is an energy-dense nutrient with 9 kilocalories per gram. Animal fat is an example of a high-quality fat source. Dogs use fats that are commonly referred to as Omega-6 long-chained fatty acids. These fats are called Omega-6 because they have a double bond at the sixth carbon atom. They are usually a mixture of saturated (solid) and unsaturated (liquid) fats. Unsaturated fat tends to turn rancid more quickly.

Another type of fat is the Omega-3 fat. Its first double chain is at its third carbon atom. Omega-3 fats have many health benefits, including anti-inflammatory qualities and decreasing the risk of developing certain kinds of tumors and cancers. These fats generally come from fish oils and linseed oils. They tend to turn rancid quickly. However, too much Omega-3 fatty acids can be dangerous. Because of their blood-thinning qualities, tests have shown that too much of Omega-3 fatty acids can inhibit blood clotting in humans (and potentially in dogs) and the potential for hemorrhaging, if injured, may be too great. Most dogs benefit from diets with no more than 4 to 5 percent of fat on a dry-matter basis coming from Omega-3s.

Carbohydrates (Grains and Veggies)

A carbohydrate is a nutrient that provides 4 kilocalories of energy per gram. Because dogs are primarily carnivores, they need much less carbohydrates than humans. In fact, AAFCO doesn't have a minimum standard for carbohydrates, which means a dog can live without them.

However, carbohydrates do play an important role, providing energy, fiber, and replacement of fuels called *glycogen* within the cells. Fiber helps in water absorption and in maintaining good bowel movements. Cooked whole grains and cooked vegetables are good sources of carbohydrates.

Definition

Glycogen is fuel used by a cell.

Vitamins

Vitamins are an important part to a dog's health as well. Here are the vitamins a dog needs to stay healthy and what they benefit:

- **Vitamin A**—Immune system, eyes, growth and repair of body tissues, skin, hair, and reproduction
- **Vitamin D**—Bones and teeth
- **Vitamin E**—Muscle, heart, blood, hormones, reproduction
- **Thiamine (B1)**—The nervous system
- **Riboflavin (B2)**—The eyes, skin, nails, nervous system, and hair

Yummy Snacks

Dogs manufacture Vitamin C in their bodies. Whether dogs can actually become deficient in Vitamin C is still debatable.

- ❧ **Pantothenic Acid**—Adrenal glands, nervous system, skin, and hair
- ❧ **Niacin**—Blood, heart, and nervous system
- ❧ **Pyridoxine (B6)**—Immune system, nervous system, and blood
- ❧ **Folic Acid**—Reproduction, blood, and bones
- ❧ **Vitamin B12**—Blood and nervous system
- ❧ **Choline**—Nervous system, blood, and bones

Besides affecting the preceding systems, vitamins often play a role in metabolic functions, such as the conversion of glucose into energy, transference of chemicals on a cellular level, and other cellular functions.

Cheese Bone Cookies

Here's a yummy biscuit my friend Anne Page so graciously let me use. It's from her paper, *Canine Classified.*

2 cups all-purpose flour
1¼ cups cheese, any kind, shredded

2 garlic cloves, minced
½ cup vegetable oil
4 TB. water

1. Preheat oven to 400°F. Combine flour, cheese, garlic, and oil, and knead well. Add water, if needed, to form stiff dough.

2. Roll out on floured surface to ½-inch thick, and cut into shapes. Place on ungreased cookie sheet. Bake 10 to 15 minutes or until bottoms are lightly browned. Cool on wire rack. Refrigerate in an airtight container.

Courtesy of *Canine Classified,* Anne Page, reprinted with permission.

Not to be used as a dog's only food.

Minerals

The minerals in a dog's diet are just as important as the vitamins. Some, like calcium, you probably have heard of. Here is a rundown of the basic minerals and what they benefit:

- ❧ **Calcium and phosphorus**—Bones and muscle. These two minerals play a crucial role together and require a ratio of approximately 1.5 (1.2 to 2.0) calcium to 1 phosphorus. If either exceeds this ratio, there can be serious problems with your dog's bones.
- ❧ **Potassium**—Nervous system, heart, and cells
- ❧ **Sodium**—Cells, water metabolism
- ❧ **Chloride**—Cells, water metabolism
- ❧ **Magnesium**—Nervous system, muscle, and bones
- ❧ **Iron**—Blood
- ❧ **Copper**—Blood
- ❧ **Manganese**—Bones and reproduction
- ❧ **Zinc**—Skin, hair, bones, muscle, and immune system
- ❧ **Iodine**—Thyroid
- ❧ **Selenium**—Bones and heart

Minerals are essential to a healthy dog's diet. However, many minerals are linked together, such as calcium and phosphorus. Excesses of one particular mineral can interfere with the absorption of other minerals and may actually cause deficiencies. Too much phosphorus in the diet in comparison to calcium will cause a calcium deficiency. Too much zinc will inhibit copper and iron, thus causing a deficiency.

This is a case where more isn't better. Keep an eye on the optimal levels of minerals (listed earlier in the AAFCO guidelines) and you most likely won't cause an imbalance.

Formulating the Diet

So now you have the basic nutrients. What do you do with them all and how do you figure out what food has what nutrients for your dog? Do you know how much protein that ground beef has and if the carrots you're giving him have enough Vitamin A?

You'll need to look up the nutritional values of foods. Because you're most likely planning on using human-grade ingredients, the USDA website www.nal.usda.gov/fnic/foodcomp/search/ is a great resource.

You know that your dog's food needs to be at least 18 percent protein on a dry-matter basis, meaning that if the food were dehydrated, it would be at least 18 percent protein. Because different foods have different water contents—especially after cooking—you'll need to adjust accordingly. How do you do that?

Dry-matter, by definition, are the ingredients with the water removed. Look in the USDA database at 80/20 hamburger cooked (100 grams). It will have the word "water" and the grams per 100 grams. Subtract the moisture from 100 percent and you have the percentage of dry-matter. Now, to

determine the protein on a dry-matter basis, take
the percentage of protein and divide it by the percentage of dry-matter.

Treats

At some point, you may throw up your
hands at the complexity of the entire thing.
Don't give up. Instead, consider creating several
types of meals and adding vitamins and mineral
supplements. That way, you can be sure your dog
gets enough variety in her diet and won't have
deficiencies.

For example, if the protein of 100 grams of hamburger is 25.75 and the moisture is 56.08, do the
following:

1. Subtract the moisture from 100. 100 minus
   56.08 equals 43.92 grams dry-matter.
2. Divide the protein by the dry-matter. 25.75
   divided by 43.92 equals .5863, or about 59
   percent protein on a dry-matter basis.

In almost all cases, it's better to work in 100-gram
increments because it's easier to do the math (25
grams out of 100 grams is 25 percent, for example).
In the case of the hamburger we just talked about,
you could feed 200 grams of food and still get 30
percent protein (if that's what you're looking for) if
you added 100 grams of hamburger. Of course, the
amount of energy is 271 kilocalories, which is not
likely to be enough for a large dog.

Microwave Dog Biscuits

½ cup all-purpose flour
¾ cup nonfat dry milk powder
½ cup quick-cooking rolled oats
¼ cup yellow cornmeal
1 tsp. sugar

⅓ cup shortening
1 egg, slightly beaten
1 TB. instant bouillon granules (beef or chicken)
½ cup hot water

1. Combine flour, milk powder, rolled oats, cornmeal, and sugar in medium bowl. Cut in shortening until mixture resembles coarse crumbs.

2. Add egg to dry mixture, and stir. Add bouillon into hot water until dissolved. Slowly pour hot water/bouillon into flour mixture with a fork until all is moistened.

3. Form dough into a ball and knead on floured board five minutes, or until smooth and elastic. Divide dough in half and roll out each half to about ½-inch thick. Make cutouts with cookie cutters, or make nuggets by rolling round into 1-inch diameter log and cutting into ½-inch pieces.

4. Arrange 6 cutout shapes or 24 nuggets on a 10-inch plate. Microwave at 50 percent power (medium) for 5 to 10 minutes, or until firm and dry to the touch. Rotate plate every two minutes and turn shapes over, halfway through the cooking time. Cool on wire rack. Shapes will crisp as they cool.

Courtesy of *Canine Classified,* Anne Page, reprinted with permission.

Not to be used as a dog's only food.

Vegetarian Dogs

Should you try to make your dog into a vegetarian? Well, it's pretty controversial because dogs are primarily carnivores (look at a dog's teeth and guts and you'll see that they're mainly for handling meat, not vegetables).

Still, some people will classify dogs as omnivores because of the occasional snacking on ruminant stomach and intestinal contents. Realistically, though, dogs eat other animals.

Can a dog live on a vegetarian diet? Well, yes, provided that all the amino acids are balanced. That may be a bit trickier if you use primarily vegetable products to provide the protein (some are poorly digested by dogs). Still, adding eggs and cheese may help balance the protein better. Many veterinary nutritionists agree with me that if you're going to feed a dog, the optimal protein source is meat.

Getting It Right—Checking Your Work

So you've figured out a cooked diet for your dog. Great! But before you start feeding it to her, it's time for one more thing—have someone who is a nutrition expert look at the diet. As much as you might be tempted to skip this step, *don't*. It's well worth your while (and your money) to make sure that what you're feeding your dog won't hurt her, either in the long or short run.

Your veterinarian can help you balance the nutrition with the aid of veterinary software, too. This is very useful because your vet can probably make recommendations as to what to add when you're in your final phases of designing your dog's diet.

The Least You Need to Know

- Dogs need a blend of protein, fat, carbohydrates, vitamins, and minerals to stay healthy.

- You can determine the nutritional content of food by searching the USDA's database and doing simple mathematics.

- Always, always have a veterinary nutritionist check your work before you start your dog on any diet.

Chapter 4

Where to Get Your Ingredients

In This Chapter

- 🦴 What kinds of ingredients do you need to buy?
- 🦴 Where to find ingredients
- 🦴 How to properly store ingredients

You've got great plans for the best dog diet ever, but now it's time to figure out where to get your ingredients and how to store them. Do you go to the local supermarket, health food store, or someplace else? In this chapter, we cover all that and more.

Regular or Organic?

Because you're making your dog's food, you've probably already decided on *human-grade ingredients*. If you're still uncertain what quality of food you should use, consider that you'll have better control over human-grade ingredients than food not fit for human consumption. While meat that's not fit for human consumption may be cheaper, you won't be able to cook it properly (at least not indoors), and the meat will have additives like charcoal or other ingredients to make sure people won't eat it.

Once you've agreed that human-grade ingredients are the way to go, the next step is to determine whether you want to use "regular" food from the grocery store or *organic* foods.

Definition

Human-grade ingredients are food items considered fit for human consumption.

Organic identifies food that is grown without pesticides, herbicides, and hormones.

If you're not worried about eating "regular" food from the grocery store, it's doubtful that you're going to be worried about feeding it to your dog. In that case, it's often easier and cheaper to get everyday food for your dog instead of much pricier organic food.

That being said, organic food, especially certified organic food, tends to taste better, in my opinion. And, arguably, organic food is better for you and your dog because it does not have hormones, pesticides, or other chemicals in it. If you're already eating organic foods, you'll probably be thinking that buying them for your dog isn't a bad idea. Problem is, it can be more expensive than if you bought regular food. But there are ways around this, too.

In a perfect world, you'd be buying organic food and cooking it for your dog. Of course, the world isn't perfect and therefore you may have to make budgetary choices. Even so, don't feel bad about it. You're buying and preparing food that you and your family could eat without much worry.

Satin Balls

A friend of mine, Charlene LaBelle, author of *A Guide to Backpacking with Your Dog* and *MUSH! a Beginners Manual of Sled Dog Training, Fourth Edition*, gave me a few recipes she uses. Her first one is used quite a bit by mushers (sled dog racers) and is very high in calories. It's good for underweight dogs, dogs who are picky eaters, older dogs, or dogs who just need a fair amount of calories. From what I understand, mushers have their own version of this recipe.

10 lbs. hamburger meat (the cheapest kind)	1¼ cups unsulfured molasses
1 large box Total cereal	10 raw eggs and shells
1 large box oatmeal	10 envelopes unflavored gelatin
1 jar wheat germ	
1¼ cups vegetable oil	Pinch of salt

Mix all ingredients together, much like you would a meatloaf. Divide into 10-quart freezer bags and freeze.

Not to be used as a dog's only food. Be very careful because this is intended to be fed raw and may harbor harmful bacteria.

Where to Shop

Your first step is to figure out where you need to shop to buy your dog's food. If you have a small dog, you'll probably buy his food from the same place you buy your own—it's easy and convenient. However, if you have a larger dog or several dogs, you may find it more difficult to feed your pet without breaking the bank.

Here are some suggestions for finding good places to buy inexpensive ingredients:

- Check the Internet. Sometimes you can get exceptional deals on products.

- Look in the phone book. Sometimes you'll find a discount place for food you didn't know about. I've found many good health food and organic suppliers this way.

- Check the big-box stores and discount clubs. Many offer discount foods—some are even organic.

- If you're buying for a large number of dogs, some meat-packing and processing facilities will sell to the public.

- Check out farmer's markets. Some will offer deals; others will be expensive.

No Biscuit!

Be careful when buying over the Internet. Buy only from reputable companies and companies whose quality you trust.

Buying in Bulk

When cooking for your dog, you're probably thinking about buying in bulk. This works, but only to a certain degree. You'll want to be careful to only buy foods that you'll be able to cook for your dog before the food becomes stale, icky, or rancid.

Buying in bulk is often the most cost-effective, but sometimes it's not. You really have to look at the price per unit because some stores will actually expect you to buy the biggest amount and price it higher to make money. Things that store well and can be bought in bulk include the following:

- Flours
- Grains (including rice)
- Dried fruits
- Nuts
- Canned items
- Frozen vegetables
- Frozen fruit
- Frozen meat (cuts, not ground)
- Oils and fat (with some caveats)

Foods that should not be bought in bulk include these:

- Dairy products: cheese and milk
- Eggs
- Fresh tofu

- Fresh fruit
- Fresh vegetables
- Fresh meat

Treats

When you're done shopping and start putting away the ingredients to your dog's food, be sure to rotate the oldest food out to the front so that you'll use it up before it gets stale.

Storing the Ingredients Properly

Once you buy your food, you're going to have to store it properly. This includes storing frozen meat, vegetables, and fruit in a freezer; fresh food in the fridge; and nuts, grains, and dried fruit in airtight containers. At this point, if you don't already have a standalone freezer, you may want to consider it. After all, once your three big dogs have their dinners in the freezer, you may not have any room for your own.

When freezing food, always be sure to double-wrap each of the items and label them well. If you have more than one dog and each one gets a different diet, be sure to put that dog's name on it, too. That way, if Rex has a beef allergy, you won't be grabbing Fifi's round steak.

No Biscuit!

Fats can become rancid over time, so it's very important to keep them refrigerated. Mark the opening date so you know when to throw them out. As a general rule, liquid fats are good in the refrigerator three months. Fats such as lard and shortening are good for eight months refrigerated.

When working with different grains and flours, it helps to put them in airtight, plastic containers to keep out weevils and other nasties. You also don't want mold or other bad things to grow in your dog's grain. Throw out any flour or grain older than a year to be on the safe side.

Although debatable, I've read that meat can stay in the freezer for a very long time. The reality is that you probably don't want to keep meat (whole or cuts) frozen longer than a year, and you don't want to keep ground meats longer than three months. Never use dairy and egg products past their expiration, just to be on the safe side. And always use cooked food within two days of cooking it.

Always use basic, safe food-handling techniques when handling raw meat. That means wearing latex or plastic gloves if you have cuts on your hands while handling raw meat, and washing utensils and plates you use with the raw meat.

Treats

One handy invention has been the disposable sealable container. These containers tend to be cheap and yet sturdy enough to hold ingredients and keep them fresh. They're also cheap enough that if you have to throw one away because it gets chewed on or gunky, you can toss it out without feeling too guilty.

Charlene's Liver Bait/Liver Greenies (Brownie) Variation 1

Charlene was kind enough to share her doggie-brownie recipes with us.

1 lb. finely ground raw liver	1 cup flour (I use whole wheat)
	½ cup cornmeal

1. Mix liver, flour, and cornmeal. Spread on a lightly greased piece of tin foil on a cookie sheet. Spread "thick." The mixture is also very thick.

2. Bake at 350°F for 25 to 45 minutes—it will depend on how thick your bait is.

3. When done baking and fully cooled, peel off the tin foil, break liver bait into pieces, and freeze in packages to fit your needs. Hint: let fully cool before putting in the bags to freeze.

Charlene makes hers really thick (approximately
1 inch thick) and uses scissors to cut it into chunks
(1×2-inch "bars"). They look like greenish brownies.
And it really does not smell all that bad.

Not to be used as a dog's only food.

Charlene's Liver Bait/Liver Greenies (Brownie) Variation 2

1 lb. liver
1 cup oatmeal
1 cup cornmeal

1 cup water (add water
as needed)

1. Use a blender to grind up liver. Add oatmeal,
   cornmeal, and water to the blender.

2. Spread on a cookie sheet that is covered with a
   piece of heavy foil. Bake at 350°F for 25 to 45
   minutes. Let cool, then cut into strips, break into
   small pieces, and put in freezer. The more water
   you add, the thinner you can make the bait.

If you use ground liver, mix in by hand. Then grind
oatmeal into "flour" before mixing together. Add
water, if needed, to mix into a thick paste. The reason you grind the oatmeal into flour is because if you
don't, the oatmeal looks like mold in the bait.

This can be frozen and refrozen. It's not greasy and
is fine for the weekend if you do not leave it in the
hot sun.

Not to be used as a dog's only food.

Dangerous Ingredients

Before you make those final plans to shop, be aware that some ingredients are too dangerous for your dog to eat. Some you may be aware of; others may surprise you. Here's a list of the nasties and why the food is dangerous to dogs:

- Chocolate—Contains theobromine, which can seriously harm the stomach, cardiovascular system, and nervous system, thus killing a dog. Dark chocolate is far more lethal than milk chocolate. (White chocolate does not contain cocoa and therefore is safe.)

- Artificial sweeteners (especially xylitol)— Can cause liver failure.

- Alcoholic beverages—Even a little can cause alcohol poisoning.

- Avocado—Contains persin, which can cause vomiting and diarrhea in dogs.

- Coffee—Contains high amounts of caffeine, which can cause stomach, cardiovascular, and nervous system problems—and even death.

- Fatty foods—Can cause pancreatitis.

- Macadamia nuts —Can cause nervous system problems including seizures, tremors, and temporary paralysis.

- Onions, onion powder, garlic, chives—Can cause hemolytic anemia.

- Raisins and grapes—In some dogs has caused kidney failure.
- Yeast dough (uncooked)—Can cause blockages and twisted intestines.
- Raw Pork—Contains trichinosis, a dangerous parasite.
- Raw salmon—Contains a dangerous parasite that can kill dogs.
- Raw game meat—May contain various worms and parasites.

Overall, any raw meat may be dangerous because it can carry various nasty bacteria such as E. coli, campylobacter, salmonella, and tularemia. Likewise, improperly handled food can carry dangerous bacteria to both you and your dog.

While edible mushrooms have not been mentioned by anyone in the know as being toxic, it has been my experience that my dogs throw up after eating even a little bit of edible mushrooms. For this reason alone, I won't give my dogs even a tiny bit. Keeping mushrooms away from dogs isn't a bad idea anyway. You don't want your dog to develop a taste for them and then eat a poisonous one in your yard.

Easy Summer Meal (for Working Dogs)

A long distance musher, Jessica Allen from Manitoba, Canada, feeds her Alaskan Huskies a simple recipe in the summertime. Be sure to add Balance-It or other supplements. The recipe needs at least ¼ cup bone meal to balance the calcium and phosphorus.

2 cups ground chicken	1 cup fat
1 cup oatmeal	½ cup ground beef liver

Mix ingredients. Add water and stir into a nice thick porridge consistency. Serve raw. Feeds two meals to a 60- to 80-lb. working dog.

This is a very high-fat diet and one I would hesitate to feed an average-weight to overweight dog, or a dog prone to pancreatitis. Still, it's another interesting diet. Be sure to add vitamins and minerals to balance it.

Not to be used as a dog's only food. Be very careful because this is intended to feed raw and may harbor harmful bacteria.

Sled Dog Snack

Jessica also has a very easy high-energy snack that rehydrates dogs as well.

Honey in squirt bottle   Liver, cut into pieces

1. Use a silicone muffin pan and squirt about 1 TB. honey in each cup. Add piece of liver.

2. Fill cups with water and freeze. (Silicone muffin pans make it easier to remove the snack.) Feed one to your dog to rehydrate her and provide a boost of energy.

Not to be used as a dog's only food. Be very careful because this is intended to feed raw and may harbor harmful bacteria.

The Least You Need to Know

- 🐾 Sometimes buying in bulk is a good deal; other times it's not.

- 🐾 There are many good sources where you can get bulk foods for your dog.

- 🐾 Be sure to know what common foods are poisonous to dogs and stay away from them.

Home-Cooked Diets

In This Chapter

- 🦴 How to feed a home-cooked diet
- 🦴 Planning meals and adding supplements
- 🦴 How to feed

You've decided that you want to cook for your dog. But how do you begin? And how do you feed your dog to ensure he's healthy once you cook up your masterpieces?

In this chapter, we cover the basics of home cooking for your dog.

Home Cooking 101

Why should you cook for your dog when there are plenty of raw diets out there? As discussed in previous chapters, home-cooked food is safer than raw food. Cooked food has less harmful bacteria and parasites that your dog (and you!) can contract.

But what about destroying the vitamins, which cooking inevitably does? And what about the work involved in cooking the food?

good

Fido's Quick Breakfast

This is an easy recipe you can make for breakfast if you run out of other food.

²/₃ c   1 cup cooked canned pumpkin or squash (no sugar added)

²/₃ c   1 cup whole cottage cheese

2 tsp. oil

Balance-It or other supplement

¹/₃ c   ½ cup sliced fruit (apples, pears, bananas, peaches)

1 hardboiled egg

Mix pumpkin, cottage cheese, oil, Balance-It, and fruit. Peel hardboiled egg and crumble on top. Good for one meal for a 60-lb. dog.

Not to be used as a dog's only food.

Vitamins are cooked out all the time in the foods we eat. That's why many of us humans tend to take multivitamins every day to compensate for our bad eating habits and for foods that we've cooked out the nutrients from. A vitamin or supplement powder should be a staple to every homemade dog food maker's larder.

But what about the work? If you're already making your dog's food, an extra step shouldn't be a big deal. If you want total convenience, you would've gone with a bag of commercial kibble and not thought much about it. Remember that by cooking the meat and eggs, you've made the food safer than if it were raw.

Treats

Here's what needs to be cooked: beef, organ meats, eggs, chicken, pork (must be cooked to avoid trichinosis), fish (salmon must be cooked to avoid a dangerous type of fluke), rabbit (must be cooked to avoid tularemia), lamb and mutton, venison and other game (must be cooked to avoid tularemia and trichinosis, depending on types of game), and grains (to aid digestion).

Liver Snaps

Cooking is a lot of fun, so why not give your dog biscuits she'll love?

3 cups wheat flour, plus extra	4 TB. oil
1 cup cornmeal	¾ cup beef or chicken broth
2 eggs beaten	1 cup cooked beef or chicken liver, diced

1. Preheat oven to 400°F. Mix flour and cornmeal. Mix eggs, oil, and broth, and add to flour mixture. Mix in liver. Add enough flour to make stiff but pliable dough.

2. Knead dough on a floured surface and roll out to ½ inch. Cut with dog biscuit cutters, and bake on greased cookie sheets for 15 minutes or until brown.

Not to be used as a dog's only food.

Treats

Here are the foods that can be fed raw: fruits, vegetables, cheeses, pasteurized milk (though some dogs are lactose intolerant), and yogurt.

Planning the Meals

Planning your dog's meals need not be complicated. Most dogs are able to do well on two meals a day, but if you wish, you can feed your dog three times a day. However, most pet owners who work find it incredibly inconvenient to rush home during their lunch hour to feed.

So how do you plan for your dog's meal? The same as you would your own. Look at the recipes and get a list of ingredients. If you're incredibly organized and able to plan ahead, you can cook a whole bunch of meals at once and then bag and freeze them for later when you don't have the time to cook for your dog.

Plan ahead at least for the week. When designing meals, choose a variety of foods. This serves several purposes. The first reason to choose a variety of foods is to avoid an imbalance. If you can feed your dog a variety of foods, there's less chance of her missing important vitamins, minerals, protein, and fat. The second reason is variety. Dogs like variety in their diet just like you do, so adding variety perks things up. The third reason is to avoid running out of a particular food. If you simply make one type of meal all the time, you may run out of it and then cause gastric distress if you feed your dog something different.

Grandma's Meat 'n' Potatoes Supper

Remember what it was like when Grandma made Sunday dinner? Your dog can have meat and potatoes, almost like Grandma made.

1 cup lean meat, roasted with juices

2 cups cooked mashed potatoes (you can use instant in a pinch)

½ cup peas and carrots

2 tsp. oil

1 tsp. bone meal

Balance-It or other supplement

Cut up cooked meat and mix with mashed potatoes and juices. Cook peas and carrots and add to mixture. Add oil, bone meal, and Balance-It. Feed when cooled. Good for a 60-lb. dog.

Not to be used as a dog's only food.

Adding Supplements

So what about supplements? I've mentioned one type of supplement, Balance-It, but there are other good supplements out there, too. What you want to make sure is that the vitamin and mineral supplements are made to balance your dog food and restore the vitamins that were cooked out. If you're concerned about the vitamins and minerals, contact a veterinary nutritionist with your dog's diet and ask them to formulate the proper supplement for your dog's diet.

You can try to add vitamins yourself, but be careful. You can oversupplement to the point of toxicity or imbalance, so watch what single vitamins you use. I always recommend a multisupplement, mainly because it's likely to be more balanced than guesswork. If you're not sure what supplements to use, talk with a veterinary nutritionist and see what he would recommend. He may have his own version of Balance-It or another supplement that he would like to see your dog use.

Woking the Dog

Did you know that dogs came from Asia originally? Let your dog celebrate his ancestral roots with something yummy!

½ cup sliced chicken	2 cups cooked rice
1 tsp. soy sauce	1 tsp. bone meal
2 tsp. oil	Balance-It or other
1 cup bok choy or Chinese cabbage	supplement

In a wok or skillet, cook chicken with soy sauce and oil. Add bok choy or cabbage and stir. Mix in cooked rice, bone meal, and Balance-It. Good for a 60-lb. dog.

Not to be used as a dog's only food.

Mandarin Oranges and Yogurt

Your dog would probably like dessert as well. Try the following:

¼ cup Mandarin oranges	1 cup plain yogurt
	1 tsp. vanilla

Mix oranges, yogurt, and vanilla; serve. Some dogs don't like the citrus taste of oranges; others do. Mandarin oranges are sweet enough that they might appeal to your pup's tastes. If it's too tart, try apples instead.

Not to be used as a dog's only food.

How Much, How Often?

So how much do you feed your dog and how often? That's really the million-dollar question here. Energy requirements for dogs vary from weight to weight, breed to breed, and even dog to dog. Each situation is going to demand different amounts of calories depending on activity level, the age of the dog (puppy, senior, lactating mom), and even the breed.

When you look at feeding your dog, look at the amount of calories he's going to ingest (you can calculate the calories by doing some simple math with the caloric values given on the USDA web-site). These values are an approximation and, as I like to say, your mileage may vary on what exactly the calories are.

No Biscuit!

Obesity is the number-one nutritional problem in dogs, just like in people. Because you're feeding your dog "the good stuff," you may go overboard and feed too much. Let your dog's shape be your guide.

Because a dog's requirements vary widely (as much as 30 percent from other dogs), your best bet is to judge your dog's health according to how she looks and feels. Having the "amazing ribless dog" is not a good thing, nor is having a dog on whom you can see every rib.

The following charts are the caloric needs for an average dog in certain situations. They should be used as a guide and *not* strictly adhered to.

Calories per day for an active dog:

10 lbs.	293 Kcals
20 lbs.	592 Kcals
40 lbs.	1,183 Kcals
60 lbs.	1,515 Kcals
80 lbs.	2,366 Kcals
100+ lbs.	2,958 Kcals

Calories per day for an inactive dog:

10 lbs.	225 Kcals
20 lbs.	455 Kcals
40 lbs.	910 Kcals

60 lbs.	1,165 Kcals
80 lbs.	1,820 Kcals
100+ lbs.	2,275 Kcals

Calories per day for puppies (under one year):

10 lbs.	540 Kcals
20 lbs.	1,092 Kcals
30 lbs.	1,632 Kcals
40 lbs.	2,184 Kcals
50+ lbs.	2,724 Kcals

So now you know how many calories you need to feed, but how often? As I've said earlier, most adult dogs need to be fed twice a day. Puppies should be fed three to four times a day in small portions because, while they need a lot of calories for their size, their stomachs aren't able to handle all that food at once.

Yummy Snacks

What is the proper weight for your dog? Well, believe it or not, one weight doesn't fit all. In fact, most weight charts aren't useful when it comes to dogs. Instead, it's better to look at your dog. He should have a tuck where his loins (and abdomen) are, and when looking at him from above, he should have a bit of an hourglass figure.

But the best way to check is to put your thumbs on your dog's spine and feel his ribs with your fingers. If you really have to press hard to feel them or can't feel them at all, your dog is too fat. Likewise, if you can see your dog's ribs and hipbones, or if there's no fat on them at all, he's probably too thin.

The Least You Need to Know

- ✄ Cooking helps kill dangerous bacteria lurking in raw meats.

- ✄ Be mindful that you will need to adjust your dog's diet so that she is neither too fat nor too thin.

- ✄ Cook your dog's food a week ahead. That way you can be sure to have all your ingredients on hand.

Chapter 6

Fresh Foods

In This Chapter

- Feeding fresh and raw foods
- How to feed raw right
- Feeding bones or bone meal

You may have heard a lot about the BARF diet or some other raw food diet. The question is whether this type of diet is right for your dog. If you believe it is, how do you feed a raw diet with any assurances of safety?

In this chapter, we talk about raw foods. Plenty of dogs eat raw diets all the time with no problems. But some don't. So we'll look at raw feeding and how to do it.

In the Raw: Why Do Raw Diets?

Raw diets—that is, feeding raw meat, bones, vegetables, and fruit—are very popular. Many people who feed their dogs raw love it. Their dogs enjoy it, and raw feeders point to their dogs' healthy coats and sudden lack of allergies with raw foods.

Treats

Freezing raw meat makes it both safer and easier to handle. When you buy your dog's meat, get it fresh, prepare the recipe, and then freeze it for later use.

Raw foods provide vitamins that would normally be destroyed with cooking or with processing. Dogs would naturally eat meat raw in the wild, along with offal, bones, and raw plants. So it makes sense to mimic the food that a dog would eat that is natural for him.

Should your dog "go raw"? There are many reasons for it, and many reasons against it, as I've discussed in earlier chapters. I won't belittle the dangers of bacteria and raw bones to you, but many dogs have eaten these diets with no ill effects, so many people discount those dangers. However, you won't be discounting them if your dog is the one who comes down with campylobacter or has a perforated intestine.

Proponents of raw diets point out that the benefits of raw food far outweigh the risks. If you feel this way, then by all means go for it. Just be certain to have your dog's diet analyzed by a veterinary nutritionist to make sure that all her nutritional needs are met, and be extra careful handling the meat.

Sashimi for Dogs

When I think raw, I think sushi and sashimi. Your dog may think so, too.

1 cup raw sushi-quality fish (no salmon), without bones

3 cups cooked brown rice

1 tsp. tamari

1 cup bok choy, Chinese cabbage, or other greens

1 tsp. oil

1 cooked egg

1 tsp. bone meal

Balance-It or other supplement

Mix all ingredients; split in half and serve. Feeds a 60-lb. dog.

This food is raw and may harbor dangerous bacteria. Not to be used as a dog's only food.

Raw Porcupines

Some people love feeding their dogs raw meat snacks. Here's one that will make your dog jump for joy.

1 lb. raw ground meat (chicken, beef, or turkey)
1 cup quick oats
1 cup bread crumbs
1 egg, slightly beaten

2 tsp. tamari or soy sauce
½ cup peas or diced carrots
1 TB. parsley

Mix ingredients and form into 2-inch balls. Freeze. When ready to give as a treat, pull one out and feed to your dog.

This food is raw and may harbor dangerous bacteria. Not to be used as a dog's only food.

Raw Liver Teriyaki

1 lb. liver   1 cup teriyaki sauce

1. Slice liver into bite-sized chunks and blot dry with a paper towel. Arrange in a bowl and pour Teriyaki sauce over it.

2. Let marinate for three to four hours in the refrigerator. Pour off excess sauce, bag in freezer bags, and put in the freezer. To serve, break off pieces and feed.

This food is raw and may harbor dangerous bacteria. Not to be used as a dog's only food.

No Biscuit!

Many raw feeders point out that dogs are fairly resistant to bacteria. While this is true, many dogs still end up sick with bacteria. The old, the very young, and those with compromised immune systems are the most at risk. One dog I know of who had been fed raw as a puppy had clostridium infections. The infections continued until the veterinarian put the dog on a hypoallergenic diet, which cleared them up. The dog is now on a commercial venison-and-potatoes diet to avoid infections. Although there's no clinical proof, I suspect the first clostridium infection occurred because the dog got sick from raw meat, and the body reacted to chicken and beef because of it.

Planning Meals

How you plan raw meals is basically up to what diet you're going to feed. With certain diets such as the Volhard diet, there are specific meals you should be making for each day. Other diets, such as whole prey diets, allow your dog to eat whenever he wants from the whole animal. Many fall somewhere in between, enabling you to have some creativity and leeway when it comes to feeding.

No Biscuit!

Never feed raw pork, game meat, or salmon to your dog. She can become very sick or even die from it due to the parasites in it.

In most cases, you'll be planning on two meals a day (unless you have a puppy, in which case, that's three meals). Plan each meal by separating the meat into meal portions, bagging it carefully, and freezing.

When handling raw meat, be sure to wear plastic or latex gloves to protect your hands from getting bacteria in cuts or into fingernail beds. Keep everything sanitized and clean when working with raw meat, and be sure to keep the raw meat frozen hard until ready to feed. Do not refreeze meat that has been thawed.

No Biscuit!

Another reason for you to be cautious when handling meat has to do with your interaction with your dog. While your dog may not get salmonella poisoning from her food even if the food was tainted, you can still indirectly get salmonella from your dog. How it works is that your dog eats the tainted food and then licks you, or maybe you play with her and fail to wash your hands before eating or touching your face. The bacteria can transfer from her to you and make you sick.

Adding Supplements

Whatever you do, don't forget to add supplements to your dog's food. This is vitally important to make sure that your dog doesn't suffer from a deficiency or imbalance. Many supplements come in pill form; others come in powder. If you supplement in pill form, either grind the pill up or hide it in a bit of meat and feed it to your dog.

Whole Bones or Not?

As if raw meat wasn't controversial enough, we're coming to a more controversial topic: raw bones. Many raw diets recommend raw bones along with the meat (such as chicken wings, meaty beef bones, fish bones with the fish, and so on). The purpose behind feeding raw bones is to provide enough calcium in the dog's diet, plus clean his teeth.

My thoughts are somewhat mixed on the issue, and proponents of the raw diets will probably chide me for my beliefs. One, it's very hard to tell how much calcium actually gets digested in a meal of bones and meat. Many bones, I suspect, while pliable enough to not cause problems, probably pass through without a lot of digestion. For those that are digested, it's hard to tell how much calcium the dog will get in relation to the phosphorus.

That being said, I have given large, raw, meaty bones to my dogs without ill effects. My dogs get a lot of calcium from those bones (their stools are often chalky), but I'm still hesitant to recommend giving raw bones to dogs because of the bacterial danger and the risks of intestinal perforations and blockages in a dog.

I recommend that if you feed raw, you at least add ground bone meal to the mix with the supplements. Studies suggest that many raw diets are low in calcium even with eating the bones. The safest thing is to have your diet tested to determine its ratio of calcium to phosphorus. That way, you can be certain that you're doing it right.

One big bonus to large bones is that large raw bones help clean teeth and gums. Occasionally, dogs chip their teeth on bones, so there is a downside to the dental benefits, but you'll have to decide if this would be a problem for your dog.

Last, I want to stress the dangers of feeding bones. *Any bones.* Cooked bones and sharp bones can be very dangerous to dogs. Bones have choked and killed dogs. They've perforated intestines and they've caused blockages. Any veterinarian can tell you horror stories about bones. Even so, many people feed raw bones without problems every day. You, as your dog's owner, will have to decide if the benefits outweigh the risks. If you're very concerned about feeding bones that are chewed and swallowed, use bone meal or calcium made from eggshell powder.

Raw Meat and Eggs Diet

This is a nice raw diet that incorporates both meat and eggs.

1 cup raw beef heart	2 eggs, hardboiled with shells on
½ cup raw lean beef	
2 cups yams, sliced or puréed	1 tsp. salt
	2 tsp. oil
2 cups potatoes, sliced, or in tiny bits made with a food processor	1 tsp. bone meal
	Balance-It or other supplement

Mix ingredients together. Divide in half. Freeze and feed. Good for two meals for a 60-lb. dog.

This food is raw and may harbor dangerous bacteria. Not to be used as a dog's only food.

How Much, How Often?

In Chapter 5, I covered the basics of caloric needs. Check out that chapter for the amount of calories your dogs need. Adult dogs need to be fed twice a day. Puppies should be fed three to four times a day.

How much meat should you feed your dog? It depends widely, which is why I refer you back to Chapter 5. A rough estimate is that small dogs, 10–25 lbs., need somewhere between $1/4$ cup to 1 cup of meat a day. Medium dogs, 25–80 lbs., need about 1 to 2 cups of meat a day. Large dogs will need over 2 cups of meat. This is a rule of thumb, and not precise. You will have to adjust the portions according to your dog.

What about bones? For the sake of argument, let's stick with bone meal because we can measure that. You need about 1 tsp. of bone meal per cup of meat to balance the calcium and phosphorus ratio.

Fat depends a lot on your dog's weight, activity level, and the amount of fat already in the meat. Fatty cuts of meat and high-fat ground beef don't need as much fat added as lean cuts do. You don't need to add much fat because fat is particularly calorie-dense; that is, it has 9 kilocalories per gram instead of the 4 kilocalories per gram of protein and carbohydrates.

Many raw feeders prefer feeding raw vegetables and fruit to feeding grains, but grains are a healthy source of vitamins, so don't discount them. Plant matter needs to make up about four times the amount of meat you feed. So if you're feeding 1 cup of meat, then feed about 4 cups of vegetables, fruits, and cooked grains a day.

You should probably consider feeding your dog eggs, but if you do, cook them. The whites in raw eggs tie up a vitamin called biotin and can cause hair loss and skin problems.

Raw Chicken Diet

While you wouldn't eat chicken livers, hearts, and gizzards, your dog will find them delectable.

1 cup ground chicken	2 tsp. oil
½ cup chicken livers, hearts, and gizzards	1 tsp. salt
	1 tsp. bone meal
1 cup diced carrots and peas	Balance-It or other supplement
2 cups cooked brown rice	

Mix ingredients together, split into two portions, and freeze. Good for two meals for a 60-lb. dog.

This food is raw and may harbor dangerous bacteria. Not to be used as a dog's only food.

The Least You Need to Know

- ❧ Be very careful when handling raw meats. Keep them frozen until ready to use.

- ❧ Many people feed raw bones with their dog's food. While many dogs eat these without problems, occasionally dogs do have difficulties with bones.

- ❧ When starting a raw diet, have a veterinary nutritionist analyze it to be sure the diet is balanced.

Chapter 7

Traveling Meals and Meals for the Sitter

In This Chapter

- What to do when you travel
- Teaching the pet sitter or boarding kennel how to feed
- Selecting a commercial diet most like yours

Your dog is on a healthy diet, but now you're going to spend two weeks on the road with your dog—how in the heck are you going to feed her? Or maybe you're going on a trip to the Bahamas and leaving your best friend behind. How are you going to get the dog sitter to cook for her? What are you going to do?

In this chapter, we cover the basics of feeding while traveling or when someone is taking care of your pet.

When You're on the Road

You've been planning a big vacation for months now. Maybe you're going to Yellowstone and planning on bringing your dog. Maybe you're going to the Bahamas and not bringing him. Whatever you're doing, you're going to have to plan your pup's meals. But it's not as easy as buying a bag of kibble and pouring it out for your dog. How can you do this?

The following are a couple of recipes you can make easily and add to any commercial food for flavor and extra nutrition.

 Ground Meat Helper for Dogs

1 lb. ground beef, chicken, or turkey
2 TB. vegetable oil or lard
1 cooked egg, diced

1 tsp. fish oil (Omega-3)
1 TB. Brewer's yeast
1 tsp. bone meal
Balance-It or other supplement

1. Cooked: Mix ground meat, vegetable oil, and egg; cook in skillet. Let cool. Mix in Omega-3 oil, brewer's yeast, bone meal, and any supplements. Mix ¼ cup helper per 1 cup kibble.

2. Raw: Mix all ingredients and form into ⅓-cup portions. Feed ⅓ cup helper per 1 cup kibble.

Not to be used as a dog's only food.

Eggs and Veggies

1 cup green, leafy vegetables such as spinach, cabbage, bok choy, kale, or other interesting vegetables	3 eggs, hard-boiled 1 TB. oil

Process leafy vegetables, eggs, and oil in a food processor. Feed ¼ cup per 1 cup of kibble.

Not to be used as a dog's only food.

Well, there's good news and bad news. The bad news is that you probably are going to have to settle for some commercial food, especially if you're traveling with your dog. The good news is that some dog foods cater to those who feed their own diets.

If you're planning on taking your dog with you, you'll probably want to pack some of his food for a shorter trip. In most cases, choose food that is easy to mix and feed—and keep. While you may have a cooler to hold your dog's food, you may discover that you don't have a big-enough cooler to hold a week to two weeks' worth of food.

What do you do if you're planning on taking your dog for longer than a few days? Or taking more than one big dog? You can do one of two things: you can buy foods at your destination and cook for your dog, or you can plan on using a certain amount of commercial food.

The first option is probably going to make your vacation into work. After all, who wants to cook for anyone when they're on their vacation, unless you're planning on camping? The second can cause gastric problems if your dog isn't slowly introduced to his new food.

Yummy Snacks

You can avoid a lot of gastric distress by slowly introducing the new food in your dog's diet. Start by adding about 10 percent of the bulk of the food to your dog's main diet (and decrease the fresh food by 10 percent). Over the next few days, increase the commercial food by 10 percent every few days while decreasing the fresh food by 10 percent. Do this until your dog is eating 50 percent fresh and 10 percent commercial and is experiencing no stomach upsets.

Choosing a commercial blend similar to your food can be a little tricky. There are plenty of dehydrated raw-food diets out there that are light and easy to pack. These foods keep fairly well. There are other types of food that are natural and are in meat rolls or other forms, which, when added with fresh fruits and veggies, make an adequate meal.

But what if someone is going to be feeding your dog at your place or at a boarding kennel—what then? You can make it simple by slowly switching over to the commercial blend and providing instructions as to how much the sitter or kennel needs to feed. Or you can do a transition diet in which you mix the commercial and some fresh foods in with your dog's normal food.

Treats

One thing you can do to make the switch easier is to have the pet sitter or boarding kennel add fresh food to your dog's diet while feeding the commercial food. That way, there should be less gastric upset and your dog will eat her meals.

Fido's Meatloaf

Who doesn't like meatloaf? Your dog will flip for this recipe, but I bet it's nothing like what Mom cooked.

1 cup oatmeal
½ cup milk
2 eggs
1 lb. ground beef, turkey, or chicken (or you can mix them)

1 cup fresh or frozen mixed vegetables diced (no onions)
¼ tsp. salt
2 tsp. bone meal
Balance-It or other supplement

1. Mix oatmeal, milk, and eggs. Let sit 10 minutes. Knead in ground meat, vegetables, salt, and bone meal.
2. Put in loaf pan and bake at 350°F or until cooked. Add vitamins and mineral supplements.

Feed according to dog's size. Not to be used as a dog's only food.

Prepackaging Food to Go

So you're planning on going on vacation. Whether you're taking your dog or leaving her at home with a pet sitter or at a boarding kennel, you'll want to be sure to have all your dog's meals planned. This requires some work on your part—and some prepackaging.

It's a good idea to prepackage the meals a week ahead of time, rather than wait until the last minute. Waiting until the last minute guarantees you'll be in a panic over packing and other planning you're doing for the trip, so avoid that if at all possible. Plus, you're bound to forget some ingredient, so having a week's time as padding will make everything easier.

Plastic zip bags and throwaway containers are your friends here. Start cooking and bagging portions for your dog and label them with a black permanent marker. Be sure to label them with the day and time, as well as your dog's name. So, for example, you should mark your dog's food like this: *Mishka, Wednesday, AM* (or the date). Take all the food and put it in your freezer so that a quick thaw in the microwave will get it to the proper temperature for cooking or serving.

Turkey Cook

Branly did not like

Here's a simple meal you can feed your dog that also freezes well.

1 lb. ground turkey	1½ tsp. salt
½ cup fat	3 tsp. bone meal
2 cups cooked barley	Balance-it or other
1 cup cooked rice	supplement
2 hardboiled eggs, diced	

Cook ground turkey in a skillet until crumbly. Remove from heat. Mix in all ingredients. Separate into two meals in plastic bags for 60-lb. dog. Freeze.

Not to be used as a dog's only food.

Giving Good Instructions

You've decided to have the kennel or your pet sitter care for your dog while you're traveling. You've checked out the facility or the sitter and are now convinced that you can trust it or him. But how do you explain how to feed your dog?

While the kennel may be very good, it's unlikely the staff's going to cook for your dog—or have lots of room for fresh foods. What's more, some kennels will actually charge more to feed food that you provide, and if it has to refrigerate or freeze the food, you will probably pay for the kennel to store it. So it's pretty much the KISS principle (Keep It Simple, Stupid) when it comes to feeding your dog. Keep everything prepackaged with written instructions for what needs to be fed when.

When giving instructions to the pet sitter, be sure that they're written down and that her work is minimal when feeding your dog. There will be less chance of a mistake that way. Always have the packages clearly labeled and marked according to the days the food is to be fed.

No Biscuit!

While many boarding kennels try to accommodate owners' requests, most can only do so much with the numbers of animals coming and going. If you really insist on feeding fresh, a better idea would be going with a pet sitter.

Cheesy Biscuits

Here's a treat you can take along while you travel and it's easy to make while on the road. You can also enjoy this treat.

2 cups flour
1 TB. baking powder
½ tsp. baking soda
½ tsp. salt
½ cup nonfat dried milk

½ cup vegetable shortening
2 TB. dried parsley or other herb
⅔ cup milk or water
1 cup grated cheese

1. Mix all ingredients except milk and cheese. Store in plastic bag for use. When you're ready, mix in milk or water and cheese until a pliable dough forms.

2. Roll out and use biscuit cutters, or flatten into a disk and cut into wedges like a pie. Bake at 350°F until brown—about 30 minutes.

Not to be used as a dog's only food.

If you go with a pet sitter, be prepared for extra cost. Most pet sitters charge per trip, so if the pet sitter comes over twice, the amount can add up quickly. Likewise, extra work means extra time spent, so a bill that might normally be $20 a day could end up over $30 a day, depending on how many trips and the amount of time spent.

Yummy Snacks

There are two national pet-sitting organizations that have listings of pet sitters in your area. Both help bond and insure their members. They include the following:

National Association of Professional Pet Sitters www.petsitters.org

Pet Sitters International — www.petsit.com

The Least You Need to Know

- You may have to supplement homemade food with commercial food if you plan on boarding your dog or have a pet sitter visit.
- You can feed a half-and-half blend of commercial food and fresh food while you travel.
- Make food packages in advance and label them clearly—it will make pet sitting and boarding easier.

Chapter 8

Scrumptious Snacks

In This Chapter

- 🦴 Treats that work with your dog
- 🦴 Making treats for your dog
- 🦴 Design your own healthy treats

If you've owned a dog for any length of time, you know that snack time is a dog's favorite time. But what treats that aren't store-bought can you give him? There are plenty of options—you just have to be creative.

In this chapter, we cover treats and snacks, including when to give your dog treats and how to design your own snacks.

Does Your Dog Really Need Treats?

Before we get started on the treat wagon, let's step back and figure out if your dog really needs treats. It might sound odd, coming from a dog food recipe book, but think about it. You're feeding your dog a homemade diet. With all likelihood, she doesn't need in-between meal snacks. And yet, if you're training your dog or if you want to give her a reward, you're looking for biscuits or a special treat.

If you're feeding your dog a complete and balanced diet, the need for treats is minimal. When feeding a homemade diet, treats are even more superfluous. How is a treat more special than her food?

Okay, maybe you want to give your dog a nice snack. Or maybe you want to train your dog to learn obedience or agility. What do you do then?

Treats

Instead of stuffing your dog full of treats, try teaching him a new trick, playing a game with him, or taking him for a walk. Your dog will enjoy it more than just a biscuit.

Well, then treats are where it's at. But before you start feeding your dog those goodies, you need to keep in mind that treats should be no more than 10 percent of your dog's total calories (unless part of her main meal is the treat).

If your dog is a little portly or you'd like to substitute something else for treats, try substituting a favorite activity. Most dogs will find it just as special (or even more special) that you played ball with them or that you took them for a walk. What's more, the exercise will be healthier for both of you.

Treats

The good news is that you can give your dog some easy treats that require no cooking. These include the following:

Popcorn, bits of plain beef jerky, Carob chips (not chocolate), tiny pieces of hotdog cut up, tiny pieces of cold cuts (turkey, ham, or roast beef) cut up, tiny pieces of cheese cut up, slices of celery, slices of carrot, unsalted peanuts, dried banana chips, pieces of dried fruit (no raisins), slices of jicama, pieces of apple, pieces of banana, pieces of rice cakes, and pieces of unsweetened cereal (puffed rice, wheat, or corn).

These treats are excellent for agility training, where you may have to use a fair amount of treats to teach the dog something. These treats are fairly low-calorie and yet enjoyable for you both.

Making Treats for Your Dog

But let's be honest here. You want to make treats for your dog. You play and exercise him enough. That's fine. Just be sure to not overfeed him treats—keep your dog's diet healthy and balanced.

Dogs love homemade treats better than store-bought. What's more, I've discovered that with the exception of the treats with raw meat in them, you can eat them, too. They're pretty tasteless, in my opinion, but they are human edible. My relatives were absolutely horrified to see me take a bite out of the biscuits I made for their dogs. It didn't seem to matter to them that everything was made with human-grade food ingredients. Maybe it was the dog-bone cookie-cutter shape. Next time I might make it with holiday patterns.

Peanut Butter Biscuits

Lots of dogs love peanut butter, so what could be a better way of showing your love than with peanut butter biscuits? They're super-easy to make and your dog will love you for it.

1 cup hot water	1 egg, beaten
1 cup nonfat dried milk	1 cup cornmeal
1 cup peanut butter (the old-fashioned organic kind)	4 cups whole-wheat flour

1. Preheat oven to 350°F. Pour hot water on nonfat dried milk and mix in peanut butter and egg. Mix cornmeal and whole-wheat flour in. Turn out onto a floured surface and knead, adding more whole-wheat flour if necessary to create a stiff dough.

2. Roll out to ½ inch and cut with bone cookie cutters. Place on a baking sheet and bake 20 to 30 minutes or until brown along the edges. Let cool and harden.

Not to be used as a dog's only food.

When you make treats for your dog, be sure to make enough of them. Because you're using no preservatives, it's a good idea to keep them in the refrigerator or even the freezer to prevent them from getting moldy. You can keep hard treats for at least six months in the freezer; if you keep them in the refrigerator, they go stale after two weeks.

What's most annoying is that the dogs know when you're baking for them (they have a second sense about such things) and will nag you until you give them a cookie.

If you don't have time and are out of treats, remember that cut celery and carrots can do in a pinch. Most dogs really love carrots and celery, and because they don't have many calories, they can be fed to your dog without too much worry.

Golden Beardie Brownies

A friend of mine, Anne Page, was the publisher of the *Houston Canine Chronicle*. When she stopped publishing it, she gave me plenty of recipes that she had printed.

1 lb. raw beef liver	1 pkg. Jiffy Corn Muffin Mix

1. Liquefy liver in a blender or food processor. Add corn muffin mix. Stir until sticky.
2. Spread on a greased cookie sheet. Bake at 350°F for 15 to 20 minutes. Allow to cool. Cut into squares and freeze.

Courtesy of the *Houston Canine Chronicle*, Anne Page, reprinted with permission.

Not to be used as a dog's only food.

Hearty Dog Biscuits

Here's another dog-biscuit recipe from the *Houston Canine Chronicle*.

1 TB. active dry yeast	2 cups fine bulgur
¼ cup lukewarm water	2 tsp. salt
2 cups lukewarm beef broth	½ cup instant nonfat dry milk
2 cups unbleached white flour	⅓ cup yellow cornmeal
2 cups whole-wheat flour	Egg wash: 1 egg plus 1 TB. water beaten

1. In a large bowl, sprinkle yeast over water, stir to dissolve, and let stand until foamy. Stir in broth. Combine flours, bulgur, salt, and dry milk. Beat mixture into yeast to make a very stiff dough.

2. Turn out onto a floured board and knead for four minutes. Divide into three equal portions; put aside two, covered with tea towel. Roll out remaining portion to the thickness of less than ¼ inch and cut with a bone-shaped cookie cutter or a small circular cutter. Place on ungreased baking sheets that have been sprinkled evenly with cornmeal. Brush cutouts with egg wash.

3. Repeat the above process with the remaining two portions of dough. Set in a warm place to rise for 45 minutes and then bake in oven preheated to 325°F for 45 minutes.

4. After all are baked, turn off oven and leave biscuits in oven overnight to harden. Store in airtight container.

Courtesy of *Houston Canine Chronicle*, Anne Page, reprinted with permission.

Not to be used as a dog's only food.

Guidelines for Creating Treats

So what makes a good treat? Good treats need to be low-fat and low-calorie. They should have little or no sugar. They should have some kind of nutritional value. And they need to be something that your dog will enjoy.

Doggie Veggies

Sometimes just plain vegetables aren't enough.

Celery cut into 2-inch pieces	Cream cheese, peanut butter, or tuna-fish salad

Spread cream cheese, peanut butter, or tuna-fish salad on the celery. Serve.

Not to be used as a dog's only food.

Most dogs will enjoy small bits of treats as much as large ones. Although many of these treats make biscuits and biscuit-shaped treats, consider making very small treats, no larger than a dime in size, so that you can give them as training-treat rewards.

When looking at human food for quick treats, think raw veggies and fruit. My dogs love peaches, and flip for tastes of yogurt. Cottage cheese makes a very healthy and satisfying snack that can also serve as part of a meal.

Remember that a treat is only good for the moment that you give it, so be very judicious about giving out treats. Your dog will probably already forget about the treat once she has eaten it, so substituting activities such as play also helps.

Yummy Snacks

There are new toys out on the market that you can fill with commercial food and leave for your dog to play with. These are puzzle toys that only dispense treats a certain way. People put kibble or treats in them to keep their dogs busy for hours.

You can use these puzzle toys as well. Fill them up with frozen peas or a combination of frozen peas and carrots. Or, if you have a food processor, put any diced vegetable or fruit you'd like to give your dog into one. Not only is it healthy, but your dog will simply love it.

The Least You Need to Know

- Choose snacks that are low in calories, fat, and sugar.
- Snacks should be no more than 10 percent of your dog's diet.
- Substitute play and exercise for treats—your dog will enjoy the quality time.

Diets for Special Needs

In This Chapter

- 🦴 How to feed a dog with allergies
- 🦴 How to feed a dog with medical conditions
- 🦴 Whether your dog should become a vegetarian

You've picked up this book hoping to come up with basic meals for your dog because your dog has a medical condition? Maybe your dog has allergies to certain types of foods such as beef or corn. Maybe your dog needs a low-fat diet. Maybe he has heart problems. Or maybe you want to share your vegan lifestyle with your pup. Regardless, you need to learn how to do that—and find out if you should.

In this chapter, we cover the basics of feeding dogs with special needs.

Yummy Snacks

Allergy or intolerance? Dogs who suffer intolerance to certain foods show it through gas, diarrhea, and digestive upset, just like people who are lactose-intolerant and can't digest milk sugar.

Allergies generally show themselves as skin problems in dogs, such as hot spots, skin infections, and itchy skin.

Dogs with Allergies and Intolerances

Your dog has never done well on store-bought food. Maybe she's been itchy and scratchy since you got her. Maybe she's had diarrhea the whole time on her current dog food. Whatever the reason, you suspect allergies.

Food allergies and intolerances are common in dogs. Dogs have shown sensitivity to protein sources such as chicken, beef, eggs, lamb, milk, and soy as well as to carbohydrate sources such as corn and wheat.

If you think your dog shows a food allergy or intolerance, talk with your vet. He can prescribe a diet with a *novel* protein and carbohydrate source, which you should feed to your dog for a minimum of 12 weeks. If your dog shows improvement, your vet can add a suspect ingredient back into the diet to see if it causes the reaction.

This is really the only conclusive way to test for allergies. Other tests, such as blood tests, aren't accurate enough.

Definition

Food that is new or normally not fed in a diet is considered **novel**.

The good news is, once you figure out what is causing the problem, you can start making your dog's food, being 100 percent certain to avoid the offending ingredients.

Fish-Bake Dinner

Because fish isn't used a lot in dog food, your dog may not have allergies to it. Some fish are more fatty than others and may not need extra oil. Avoid over-using tuna, as it has a higher level of mercury in it than many other kinds of fish. This recipe is good for dogs with corn and wheat allergies as well.

1 lb. fish (any variety)	1½ tsp. salt
¼ cup vegetable oil	3 tsp. bone meal
2 cups cooked barley	Balance-It or other
1 cup cooked oatmeal	supplement
2 hardboiled eggs, diced	

1. Broil fish in oven under a broiler. Turn once until fish is flakey and done. Remove from oven and let cool.
2. Remove bones, and flake fish into bowl. Mix in all ingredients. Separate into two meals into plastic bags for 60-lb. dog. Freeze.

Not to be used as a dog's only food.

Diets for Certain Protein and Grain Allergies

So you find out from the veterinarian that your dog is allergic to chicken, beef, or even the so-called hypoallergenic lamb (that really isn't hypo-allergenic). What do you feed your dog?

No Biscuit!

Lamb and rice used to be touted as the great hypoallergenic diet—until everyone started using it. Vets used to recommend lamb and rice because lamb was a novel protein source. Breeders and dog owners thought that this was a magic bullet to skin problems, and began feeding it in great quantities. Soon, dogs began showing allergic reactions to—you guessed it—lamb.

Well, you go with protein sources that your dog isn't allergic to, such as cooked pork, rabbit, or fish. (Feeding game meat to dogs is often illegal in many states). You must first know your dog's allergies because otherwise you may be simply feeding the same ingredients (better ingredients, but the same that caused the problem). Once you have a handle on your dog's allergies, you can start feeding him foods from other protein sources.

What about dogs who are allergic to grains? Many dogs have allergies to corn and wheat, so you'll have to be on guard for those ingredients. Wheat and corn crop up everywhere—even in human foods, so be careful. Many health-food stores have good wheat substitutes. Consider potato flour, rice flour, chickpea flour, soy flour, oat flour, and barley flour as possible substitutes. Experiment with the recipes here and any others you get from other books and the Internet. You can make easy substitutions with different flours if your dog is allergic to wheat or corn.

Treats

When considering your dog's allergies, consider that she may be allergic to more than just the meat of the animal, including the fat. Be sure to use a different fat than from the animal she's allergic to.

Peanut Butter Biscuits

Your dog loves peanut butter biscuits, but he's allergic to wheat and corn. What can you do? Substitute, of course! Here's the recipe with substitutions for wheat and corn.

1 cup hot water	2 cups brown rice flour
1 cup nonfat dried milk	1 cup soy flour (or 1 cup rice flour)
1 cup peanut butter (the old-fashioned organic kind)	1 cup oatmeal
1 egg, beaten	

1. Preheat oven to 350°F. Pour hot water on nonfat dried milk and mix in peanut butter and egg. Mix in flours and oatmeal. Turn out onto a floured surface (using rice flour) and knead, adding more whole-wheat flour if necessary to create a stiff dough.

2. Roll out to ½ inch and cut with bone-shaped cookie cutters. Place on a baking sheet and bake 20 to 30 minutes or until brown along the edges. Let cool and harden.

Not to be used as a dog's only food.

Feeding Dogs with Medical Problems

Your dog has a heart condition. Or maybe it's kidney problems. Or maybe she has liver problems. You know she needs to be on a strict diet—your vet advises it. How do you feed her?

Easy Biscuits for Dogs Allergic to Corn and Wheat

My dogs love this easy biscuit recipe. It's simple to make and is made with human-quality ingredients that you can eat, too, if you're so inclined.

1 stick butter or mar-
garine
1 cup boiling hot water*
3 cups rice flour or
potato flour
1 cup oatmeal (steel-cut
variety)

1 cup nonfat dried milk*
1 tsp. tamari (without
wheat)
1 egg
1 TB. dried parsley
(optional)

*You can substitute 1 cup goat's milk heated in the microwave and ¼ cup rice flour for nonfat dried milk and hot water.

1. Preheat oven to 350°F. In a large bowl, mix butter and hot water until dissolved. Add flour, oatmeal, and nonfat dried milk. Mix well. Add egg and parsley, and mix. Dough should be thick but not dry. Add extra flour or water as needed and knead with hands.

2. Roll dough out on rice or potato-floured surface and cut with bone-shaped cookie cutter. Put on ungreased cookie sheet and bake one hour until bottom is browned or until hard. Remove and cool. Store in airtight containers.

Not to be used as a dog's only food.

Dogs who have medical conditions can be fed home-cooked food, but this is something that is beyond the scope of this book. A sick dog needs precise nutrition to help maintain her health with her current condition. Talk with your veterinarian or contact a veterinary nutritionist on what diets will be right for your dog. You may find that with some modifications, the diets within this book might be acceptable to feed. But don't chance it. Talk with your veterinarian about creating meals that will help keep your dog healthy.

Veggie Stir-Fry

Not a complete diet, but a nice change of pace from meat. Your dog will enjoy the crunchy texture.

2 eggs, slightly beaten	2 tsp. tamari (no wheat added)
1 lb. semi-firm tofu, cut into cubes	2 tsp. oil
1 cup bok choy	3 cups cooked brown rice
½ cup water chestnuts, sliced	2 tsp. bone meal
½ cup bamboo shoots	Balance-It or other supplement
½ cup carrots and peas	½ cup peanuts

1. Cook eggs in a nonstick pan so they come out like a pancake. Remove, cool, and slice into strips. Stir-fry tofu, bok choy, water chestnuts, bamboo shoots, carrots, peas, tamari, and oil in a wok.

2. Mix rice, bone meal, and Balance-It. Mix stir-fry with rice. Add peanuts and egg. Split in half. Will feed two meals to a 60-lb. dog.

Not to be used as a dog's only food.

Vegetarian Dogs?

If you're a vegetarian or a vegan, you may think that feeding your dog a vegetarian or vegan diet is a good idea. However, this isn't necessarily so. While dogs can and have subsisted on vegetarian diets, don't fool yourself into thinking that dogs would rather eat vegetables over meat. Dogs are carnivores, not omnivores, and while not as strictly carnivorous as cats, their bodies are built for eating and digesting animal products.

It doesn't necessarily mean that you can't share your meals with your dog from time to time, but be aware that a dog's body functions best with high-quality protein derived from meat, not from plants.

If you choose to feed your dog a vegetarian diet, I would highly recommend that you consult with a veterinary nutritionist to be certain that your dog is getting all the right amino acids and fats he needs in his diet.

Pasta Supper Bake

1 lb. ricotta cheese
1 lb. cottage cheese
2 eggs, slightly beaten
3 tsp. salt
3 tsp. bone meal
3 small zucchini, sliced
½ cup fresh basil
½ cup fresh parsley,
snipped into small
pieces

2 cups mozzarella
3 cups cooked whole-
wheat* pasta
½ cup parmesan cheese
Balance-It or other
supplement

*You can substitute rice pasta

1. Mix ricotta and cottage cheese with eggs, salt,
   bone meal, zucchini, basil, and parsley. Add
   1 cup mozzarella and blend thoroughly. Stir
   in cooked noodles and pour into a deep dish.
   Sprinkle with rest of mozzarella and parmesan
   cheese.

2. Bake at 350°F until bubbly. Sprinkle Balance-It
   or vitamins and minerals on top and let cool.
   Should make three meals for a 60-lb. dog.

Not to be used as a dog's only food.

Pan-Fried Potatoes

A nifty treat, because most dogs love roast potatoes. You can substitute yams or sweet potatoes for the regular potato.

1 large potato, sliced	1 tsp. sesame seeds
1 tsp. canola oil	¼ tsp. sea salt

Put potato slices and canola oil in a frying pan and cook on high until browned. Turn off and add sesame seeds and salt. Let cool and serve.

Not to be used as a dog's only food.

The Least You Need to Know

- ✤ Your veterinarian can determine what allergies or intolerances your dog has and can help you design a diet for your dog.

- ✤ Dogs with medical conditions need to be fed very specific diets. Consult a veterinary nutritionist to help you develop a diet for your dog.

- ✤ While dogs enjoy fruits and vegetables, don't make your dog into a vegetarian. It's not normal for them.

Troubleshooting Diets

In This Chapter

- 🦴 Recognizing dietary problems
- 🦴 Simple fixes for possible diet problems
- 🦴 Learning when to call in an expert when there's a health problem

You've created your own diet for your dog and have been feeding it for some time. But something is wrong. Your dog isn't as healthy as he should be. He has diarrhea or maybe his hair-coat isn't good. Or something else is wrong.

Don't panic. In this chapter, we discuss possible health problems due to diet and what you can do to remedy them.

Is It the Diet?

You've been feeding your dog his homemade diet for some time and you've noticed that he's not as healthy as he should be. Maybe he's itchy and has skin and coat problems. Maybe he has a bunch of gastric distress. Maybe he has diarrhea and vomiting.

Yummy Snacks

Most diets take six weeks or more before you can actually see the results, either positive or negative. However, results may show up almost immediately if your dog has an abrupt change in diet, a diet with irritating ingredients such as bones, a diet with contaminating bacteria, or a diet that includes foods your dog has an intolerance for.

Before you start making changes to your dog's diet, schedule an appointment with your veterinarian and have your dog thoroughly checked out. That means an exam and blood work, not to mention a stool sample to check for parasites. Dogs can get sick for a variety of reasons—diet is just one factor. Be sure your dog doesn't have any infections or other conditions that could be causing him to get sick. This is vitally important because your dog may be sick with a disease or condition that may be life-threatening if not taken care of.

If your dog checks out okay, then talk to your veterinarian about your dog's diet. If it's a diet that your veterinarian (or veterinary nutritionist) recommended or balanced properly for you, you may have to ask her to look for things such as deficiencies or allergies to particular foods.

Sadie's Chicken Livers

A friend of mine has a mixed breed who loves this recipe of cooked chicken livers. It freezes well and you can serve a chicken liver right from the freezer to your dog's bowl along with her food.

1 cup fresh raw chicken livers
¼ cup olive oil

1 garlic, pressed (optional)

1. Sauté chicken livers in a frying pan with olive oil and garlic. (Throw out the garlic when done). Cook thoroughly.
2. Cool and put in plastic bags, and keep in the freezer.

Not to be used as a dog's only food.

If your dog does indeed have deficiencies or allergies, you may have to seriously evaluate what you are feeding and why your dog isn't getting the proper nutrition. At this stage, it's time to switch to a super-premium commercial food your vet recommends and then work with a veterinary nutritionist who will test the diet to be sure it at least meets the AAFCO minimums.

Lamb and Rice Supper

Although no longer considered hypoallergenic, you can still feed lamb and rice to your dog.

1½ cups ground lamb
2 tsp. olive oil
1 cup diced eggplant
1 hardboiled egg, diced
2 tsp. bone meal

1 tsp. iodized sea salt
4 cups cooked rice
Balance-It or other supplement

Sauté lamb in olive oil. Add eggplant and cook until softened. Remove from heat and let cool. Add egg, bone meal, salt, rice, and Balance-It. Divide into two portions. Makes two servings for a 60-lb. dog.

Not to be used as a dog's only food.

Jerky for Dogs

You can make your own jerky for your dog to enjoy. Try this simple recipe:

1 lb. lean chicken, turkey, pork, or beef brisket, sliced into thin slices.

1 cup teriyaki sauce or soy (tamari) sauce

Dip pieces of meat into sauce and put in dehydrator, dehydrating trays, or on the oven rack with a tray below to catch juices. Arrange pieces so they do not touch. Bake 12 hours at 150°F.

Not to be used as a dog's only food.

Diarrhea/Gastric Distress

Diarrhea is often one of the first symptoms dog owners see their dogs experience when changing diets. If your dog has diarrhea and gas, you may be changing the diet too quickly. Another reason for diarrhea is possible bacterial contamination of raw meat and eggs. In this case, the dog's gut is reacting to the infection and is trying to fight it by getting rid of the offending food.

Treats

If your dog is new to the diet and reacts, try switching her back to her old food. In many cases, if your dog has diarrhea or vomiting, switching back may eliminate the problem. If it does, you may then want to slowly add the new food back in by 10 percent each day.

Diarrhea can be very serious, so don't discount it. It can quickly lead to dehydration and electrolyte imbalances. Likewise, gas can lead to bloating—a serious condition in large, deep-chested breeds that can lead to death. Bring your dog to a vet as soon as possible.

Diet for an Overweight Dog

Before using this diet, check with your veterinarian to make sure your dog should be on such a diet.

1 cup lean ground chicken or turkey

1 cup low-fat cottage cheese

2 tsp. olive oil

2 cups zucchini, yellow squash, or pumpkin

2 cups cooked brown rice

3 tsp. bone meal

2 tsp. salt

Balance-It or other supplement

Broil the ground chicken or turkey and drain off fat. Break into pieces and mix with other ingredients. Makes three meals for a 60-lb. dog.

Not to be used as a dog's only food.

Bloody Diarrhea/Vomiting

Bloody diarrhea is a serious condition and one that should only be treated by a veterinarian. It can sometimes occur due to irritation of the bowels from bones and other rough objects. Bacteria and viruses can also cause bloody diarrhea.

Some people will tell you that severe diarrhea, vomiting, and other health-related issues are a type of detoxification. Don't believe that for a moment. Dogs who are getting sicker on a diet aren't necessarily going to get well. If your dog has diarrhea, bloody diarrhea, or vomiting, these conditions can lead to dehydration and electrolyte imbalances that can be life-threatening. Bring your dog to the vet at once!

Vomiting is not necessarily an emergency unless your dog vomits more than once, projectile vomits, or vomits stuff that looks like coffee grounds. Each of these signifies a serious condition.

No Biscuit!

Don't feed only meat to your dog. Although dogs are carnivores, muscle meat alone does not provide enough calcium to balance the phosphorus in meat. Dogs who are fed all-meat diets quickly lose bone mass and suffer crippling deformities and severe fractures. This is why I always try to include bone meal with foods that have meat. The bone meal will properly balance the phosphorus in the meat a dog eats.

Constipation

Dogs who are constipated often don't have enough fiber in their diets. If your dog has mild constipation, try mixing a small amount of psyllium powder in with her food each day. Psyllium can be bought at drug stores. Be sure to buy the unsweetened and unflavored versions and be sure to mix it with food. Extreme constipation may require a vet's intervention.

Poor Hair-Coat/Scratching

Poor hair-coat and scratching from itchy skin usually occur weeks into the diet, if at all. They can suggest food allergies, worms, external parasites, lack of oils in diet, and other causes not related to food, such as hypothyroidism, cancer, Cushing's disease, and autoimmune problems. A trip to the veterinarian is in order.

Obesity

Obesity is the number-one nutritional problem in pets. Basically, you're feeding your dog too much. It's not hard to do, especially when dogs love homemade food. However, there are times when your dog may be fat due to a medical condition such as hypothyroidism. This is why a quick trip to the vet is in order.

In many cases, this isn't the case. Substituting canned pumpkin and fresh vegetables for fat will help your dog slim down, as will an exercise program. Consult your vet for making changes to your dog's diet and recommendations for an exercise program.

No Biscuit!

When increasing your dog's food, especially fat and protein, you want to be very careful and do it gradually over time. Many dogs' systems can't handle that much fat, protein, and calories all at once, and it will cause them to have diarrhea and gastric problems. Add a little more at each meal and let your dog get acclimated to it.

Underweight

Most dogs are overweight, so when you see an underweight dog, he stands out. In most cases, slowly increasing your dog's protein and fat is enough to increase his weight.

Have your vet examine your underweight dog, especially if he's not gaining weight. Problems such as internal parasites or cancer may be causing him to keep the weight off.

Doggie Ice Cream

Who doesn't enjoy ice cream on a hot afternoon? Why leave your dog out of the fun? The problem with ice cream is that it's full of sugar, and it upsets dogs' stomachs because they're lactose-intolerant. Here's an easy way around that.

2 cups Lactaid milk	1 tsp. vanilla

Warm milk to almost boiling and mix in vanilla. Pour into ice-cube molds and freeze. Pop out a treat on a hot summer day.

Not to be used as a dog's only food.

Picky Dog

With homemade diets, you almost never have a picky dog. However, if you do, it's time to have your dog visit your veterinarian. Pickiness suggests a reason not to want to eat, such as dental and mouth problems, stomach problems, and other related reasons.

No Biscuit!

If your dog normally has a good appetite and stops eating, or if your dog is picky, it may suggest an underlying problem. Bring your dog to a veterinarian for a thorough checkup.

Bad Breath

Bad breath is usually a sign of dental problems or other serious health problems. If your dog's breath isn't sweet smelling, it's time for a trip to the vet and the doggie dentist!

The Least You Need to Know

- Health problems are often caused by other things besides diet.

- If your dog is showing a health problem, a trip to the veterinarian is warranted.

- Feeding a meat-only diet can cause serious imbalances that can cause bone fractures and even death.

Glossary

AAFCO The Association of Animal Feed Control Officials is made up of veterinarians, state feed control officials, and pet food manufacturers who have developed guidelines for nutritional adequacy in pet foods.

amino acids Building blocks that make up protein.

calorie A calorie is a measure of energy. It is the energy required to raise the temperature of a gram of water by 1° Centigrade.

complete protein source A source of protein that contains all 10 essential amino acids.

dry-matter basis The percentage or amount of nutrient as compared to the overall weight of the food without water.

essential amino acids Amino acids that must be present in a dog's diet to prevent a deficiency.

FDA The U.S. Food and Drug Administration is the federal government's regulatory agency that supervises food, animal feed, and medications for safety in the United States.

glycogen   Fuel used by a cell.

human-grade ingredients   Food that is considered fit for human consumption.

incomplete protein source   A source of protein that contains only nine or less of the essential amino acids.

kilocalorie   A kilocalorie is the energy required to raise the temperature of a kilogram of water by 1° Centigrade.

nonessential amino acids   Amino acids that are manufactured within a dog's body.

novel   Food that is new or normally not fed in a diet.

organic   Food that is grown without pesticides, herbicides, and hormones.

wheat gluten   A type of protein derived from wheat.

Websites

AVMA—www.avma.org The website for the American Veterinary Medical Association.

Balance-It—www.balanceit.com This website sells nutritional supplements and balancing software for veterinarians.

Dr. Ian Billinghurst—www.drianbillinghurst. com Dr. Billinghurst is the creator of the BARF (Biologically Appropriate Raw Food) diet.

FDA—www.FDA.gov The Food and Drug Administration lists recalls and other food-related information.

National Association of Professional Pet Sitters—www.petsitters.org A place to find professional pet sitters.

Pet Sitters International—www.petsit. com Another place to find professional pet sitters.

The Volhard Diet—www.volhard.com Volhard's training and diet website.

USDA—www.usda.gov This is a useful government website that deals with anything agricultural. It's a great resource.

USDA Nutritional website—www.nal.usda. gov/fnic/foodcomp/search A place to find nutritional information.

Appendix C

Recipes

Carob Treats

Yield: 2 to 3 dozen

3 cups whole-wheat flour
2½ cups oatmeal
½ cup powdered milk
½ cup wheat germ
1 TB. brown sugar

⅛ cup corn oil or margarine or butter
2 oz. carob chips, melted
1 cup water
¼ cup molasses
⅛ cup peanut oil

1. Mix whole-wheat flour, oatmeal, powdered milk, wheat germ, and brown sugar in a large bowl. Add remaining ingredients and mix until blended. Dough will be stiff. Chill.

2. Roll dough onto a greased cookie pan, and cut into shapes ½-inch thick. Bake at 300°F for one hour.

Not to be used as a dog's only food.

Cheese Nugget Dog Treats

1½ cups hot water or meat juices
1 cup uncooked oatmeal
¼ cup margarine or butter
½ cup powdered milk

1 cup grated cheddar cheese
¼ tsp. salt
1 beaten egg
1 cup cornmeal
1 cup wheat germ
3 cups whole-wheat flour

1. Pour hot water over oatmeal and margarine or butter, let stand five minutes. Stir in milk, cheese, salt, and egg. Add cornmeal to wheat germ. Mix well. Add flour ½ cup at a time. Knead for three to four minutes. Add flour until dough is stiff.

2. Roll out ½-inch thick and cut into shapes. Bake on greased sheet for one hour at 300°F. Turn off heat and leave in oven for an hour and a half.

Not to be used as a dog's only food.

Sharon's Liver Cake Cookies

1 lb. cooked mashed
chicken livers
½ cup cornmeal

2 TB. garlic
1 cup whole-wheat flour

Mix all ingredients. Dough will be soft and sticky.
Spread dough on a cookie sheet and bake at
350°F until dry. Break into pieces.

Not to be used as a dog's only food.

Canine Cookie Bones

1 lb. beef liver
2 cups water
1½ cups toasted wheat germ

1½ cups whole-wheat flour

1. In a 2-quart pan, bring liver and water to boil over high heat. Cover and simmer over reduced heat, until liver is no longer pink in the center, approximately 10 minutes. Pour through strainer over a bowl, reserving 1 cup of the liquid. Cut liver into 1-inch pieces.

2. Put liver in a blender or food processor; whirl, and add reserved liquid until smoothly puréed. Scrape into a bowl. Stir in wheat germ and flour until well moistened.

3. On a lightly floured board, roll out dough to ½-inch thickness for large bones. Cut with cookie cutter.

4. Place bones 1½ inches apart on a greased baking sheet. Bake in 350°F oven until browned, about 20 minutes. Turn off heat and leave in the oven at least three hours.

5. Refrigerate in an airtight container up to two weeks; freeze for longer storage. Makes approximately 7 large bones, 11 medium bones, or 46 small bones.

Not to be used as a dog's only food.

Index